The Story *of* Redemption

VOLUME 3 • PROVERBS - MALACHI

KRISTIN SCHMUCKER & MIRANDA EWING

Contents

the fear of the Lord

Proverbs

GENRE: *Wisdom, Poetry*

AUTHOR / DATE WRITTEN

Various, namely Solomon • c. 900 BC

KEY VERSE

PROVERBS 1:7

The fear of the Lord is the beginning of knowledge;
fools despise wisdom and discipline.

Proverbs 1-3

From the start of Proverbs, the goal of the book is clear: to know wisdom and become wise.

"As we read Proverbs, we can picture Jesus as our counselor and instructor, leading us to truth."

Solomon, the son of David and king of Israel, is the author of most of the Proverbs. He was famous for having "wisdom and understanding beyond measure" (1 Kings 4:29 ESV). And while Solomon was one of the wisest men who ever lived, his wisdom is but a shadow of the all-surpassing wisdom we find in Jesus. Jesus is the embodiment of wisdom (1 Corinthians 1:24), so as we read Proverbs, we can picture Jesus as our counselor and instructor, leading us to truth.

Proverbs is divided into two main sections. The first nine chapters introduce the entire book and include ten speeches from Solomon to his son. There are also four poems in which wisdom is personified as "Lady Wisdom." This introduction to Proverbs highlights that the fear of the Lord is the beginning of all wisdom (Proverbs 1:7). This fear is not the "terror" of the Lord, but rather awe and worship of who He is. When we have this disposition toward the Lord, we desire to walk in obedience to Him. We will want to follow the wisdom of Proverbs when we worship God rightly. The second section includes chapters 10-31. These chapters contain all of the proverbs and sayings and cover a wide variety of topics. It is important to note that Proverbs is wisdom literature, so the sayings in Proverbs are general wisdom, meaning they are not absolute promises to us.

In the first chapter of Proverbs, Solomon encourages his son not to entangle himself with the wicked (Proverbs 1:15). These men wait to shed blood to gain for themselves (Proverbs 1:11-13). This is the opposite of how Christ lives and calls us to live. He lays down His life for us and sheds His own blood so that we may be cleansed, and He calls us to lay down our lives for others (John 10:17-18, 1 John 3:16).

In chapter 2, Solomon teaches his son the value of wisdom. He tells him to seek wisdom like "hidden treasure" (Proverbs 2:4). This reminds us of Jesus's teaching about the kingdom of heaven being like a hidden treasure in a field, and when a man finds the treasure, he sells everything he has in order to own the field in which it is buried (Matthew 13:44).

Finally, in chapter 3, Solomon focuses his instruction on living in obedience to the Lord. He tells his son to "trust in the Lord" and "fear the Lord," and he shows him that blessing will result from following and loving God. He encourages him to live a life of humility, which reminds us of Christ, our perfect example of humility (Proverbs 3:34). Christ has all wisdom, but he also has all humility, which shows us that these two things go hand in hand. Ultimately, Proverbs will shows how we can pattern our lives after our Savior.

QUESTIONS

Meditate on Proverbs 1:7. How does this verse help prepare your heart for the wisdom within Proverbs?

Read Proverbs 2:6, and then read James 1:5. How do these verses compel you to ask for wisdom?

Chapter 3 begins with a warning to a son not to forget the godly wisdom his father is giving him. Do you find it easy to forget the godly wisdom the Bible has for us? What are some practical ways you can remember the wisdom of the Lord?

Proverbs 4-6

As Solomon continues to speak directly to his son, he reminds him that pursuing wisdom is a family tradition.

"The Word of God will direct our steps."

David instructed Solomon, and now Solomon instructs his own son. Likewise, if we believe in the forgiveness of our sins through the power of the death and resurrection of Christ, we are God's adopted sons and daughters (Ephesians 2:8-9, 2 Corinthians 5:21). And as such, we are to seek the wisdom of our Father. Solomon urges his son to "get wisdom" and tells him that "it is your life" (Proverbs 4:5, 13). Do we seek after the wisdom that is ours in Christ? He is the very Word of God incarnate—the source of all wisdom. He has become our life (John 1:14, Colossians 3:4). Solomon distinguishes the path of the wicked and the path of the righteous to his son. The path of the righteous will only become brighter and brighter as the redeemed move toward eternity with Him, but the wicked do not even understand that they are stumbling in the darkness. (Proverbs 4:18-19, 2 Corinthians 3:18, Revelation 22:5).

In chapter 5, Solomon warns his son specifically against sexual sin. He urges his son that a woman who involves herself in adultery is not concerned about the path that leads to life (Proverbs 5:6). When we engage in sexual sin, we focus on our present desires in this life instead of setting our minds on the things above (Colossians 3:1-2). We forget that sex was a beautiful gift designed for marriage and that marriage itself is a picture of the gospel. When a husband loves "the wife of [his] youth," he imitates Christ, who perfectly loved His bride, the church, by laying down His life for her (Ephesians 5:25). Jesus has always been faithful to His people. Solomon warns his son that everything we do is on display before the Lord. This should comfort us because our God is so near, but it also serves as a reminder to us that our sin is not hidden (Proverbs 5:21). And while we all could describe ourselves as once being "tangled in the ropes [our] own sin," God has graciously redeemed us and forgiven us through the work of Christ (Proverbs 5:22, 2 Timothy 1:9).

Solomon gives His son practical warnings against being in debt and laziness in chapter 6. Both of these things can easily creep into the life of a believer. They prohibit us from giving ourselves entirely to the good work of the kingdom of God. While works do not save us, our money, time, and energy are all used by the Lord for His glory (1 Corinthians 15:58). We do everything unto the Lord (Colossians 3:23). Solomon also warns his son again against

adultery, and he tells him to keep his father's commandments close and to meditate on them wherever he goes (Proverbs 6:20-23). A similar command is mirrored in the New Testament as we are told to let the Word of God dwell in us richly and to abide in Jesus, the living Word of God (Colossians 3:16, John 15:4-5). The Word of God will direct our steps, and as we struggle with the temptation to sin, we can remember that Jesus is near to us and ask Him to give us His strength and wisdom.

QUESTIONS

Reread Proverbs 4:25-27. Then read Hebrews 12:1-2. On what should we fix our eyes, and what path should we follow?

Focus on Proverbs 5:12-13. Spend some time in self-examination. Do you find that you tend to hate correction and discipline? In what ways is discipline good for us?

What does Proverbs 6:27-28 tell us about our sinful nature?

Proverbs 7-9

In chapter 7, Solomon focuses again on preparing his son to face sexual temptation.

He knows that this kind of temptation will inevitably occur, and he wants him to be ready with wisdom. Solomon gives his son a specific example of what adultery looks like and reminds him that following this sin leads to death (Proverbs 7:23, 27). He encourages his son to keep his commandments and teaching close to remind himself of them constantly (Proverbs 7:1-3). We are all naturally susceptible to sin. And though our desire for immediate pleasure can be fierce, God's way is better! He does not withhold any good thing from us (Psalm 84:11). He has designed us for sex, but He wants us to experience it in a way that is holy, safe, and beautiful. As we struggle with sin, we can take comfort in knowing that we have Jesus, and we can cry out to Him in our weakness (Hebrews 4:14-16).

In chapter 8, Solomon contrasts the call of the adulteress to the call of wisdom. We are faced with both of these calls in our time here on earth, and we need to ask ourselves which call we are mostly listening to. When we remember that Jesus is the embodiment of wisdom, we can attribute many of the words in this chapter to Him. Jesus speaks only what is righteous, just like Lady Wisdom (Proverbs 8:6-7). Jesus's instruction and knowledge are better than all silver and gold (Proverbs 8:10-11). He loves those who love Him, and those who seek Him will find Him (Proverbs 8:17). Jesus gives His followers a rich inheritance by allowing them to become co-heirs with Him to the kingdom of God (Proverbs 8:21, Romans 8:17). He was there before the foundation of the world, as was His wisdom (Proverbs 8:22-31). Blessed are those who keep Christ's ways (Proverbs 8:32)! Whoever finds Christ, finds life!

In chapter 9, Solomon closes his introduction to the book of Proverbs and his speeches given directly to his son. He again challenges his son to decide if he will follow wisdom or folly. When Solomon describes the invitation of Lady Wisdom in Proverbs 9:5-6, we can hear the echo of Jesus saying to His disciples, "Come and you'll see" (John 1:39). When we follow Jesus and imitate Him, we leave our simple ways and find abundant life. Truly, "The fear of the Lord is the beginning of wisdom, and the knowledge of the Holy One is understanding" (Proverbs 9:10). These words are the foundation of the book of Proverbs, and they encourage us to urgently pursue our Savior. He is where all wisdom can be found.

"When we follow Jesus and imitate Him, we leave our simple ways and find abundant life."

QUESTIONS

Meditate on the imagery used in Proverbs 7:3-4. What does this tell you about the importance of holding tightly to wisdom?

Reread Proverbs 8:11. Do you count wisdom as more valuable than riches? Do you desire earthly things above wisdom?

After reading Proverbs 9, compare and contrast wisdom and folly. Why is it important to know the difference?

Proverbs 10-12

These chapters begin the second section of Proverbs, which is full of short, two-phrase wisdom sayings, typically one verse long.

As we read them slowly and meditate on them in our minds and hearts, we will know and love wisdom. Many topics are addressed in the book of Proverbs, and while we will not be able to cover each saying in-depth, we will highlight some of the proverbs that uniquely point us toward Christ.

Solomon illustrates again and again how the righteous will be blessed. We deserve to be grouped with the wicked and foolish, but Jesus has united us with Himself. What is true of the righteous is true of us because of Christ (1 Corinthians 1:30). For example, we have access to the God of the universe now, and He has become our Father! He cares for us and lavishes blessings upon us (Proverbs 10:3, 22). We also have received true life, and God will not permit us to be moved (Proverbs 10:16, 30).

Furthermore, our faith in Christ allows us to live out Solomon's proverbs on the power of the tongue and our words. When we are in Christ, we seek to imitate Him in how we speak (Colossians 3:16). Solomon describes the words of the righteous as a "fountain of life" and like "pure silver" (Proverbs 10:11, 20). One of the most noticeable differences in the life of those who decide to follow Jesus is that they begin to speak like Him; their words are full of "grace and truth" (John 1:14).

In chapter 11, Solomon urges his son, again and again, to live in righteousness. In verse 20, we find a description of ourselves before and after being saved by Christ. We once had "twisted minds" and were "detestable" to the Lord because of our sin, but now we have become "blameless" and are a "delight" to Him. When the Lord looks on us, He sees His Son. We are new creations in Jesus (2 Corinthians 5:17). In verse 21, we see a hint of the fulfillment of the first promise of the coming Messiah from Genesis 3:15. The serpent's offspring will be dealt a fatal blow to the head—they will not go unpunished. Contrastingly, the women's offspring, the redeemed people of God, will be delivered by Christ. Another reference to the beginning chapters of Genesis is in verse 30. The fruit the righteous produce from their lives is compared to the tree of life, which represents God's presence (Genesis 2:9,

"When we are in Christ, we bear fruit that represents God to the world."

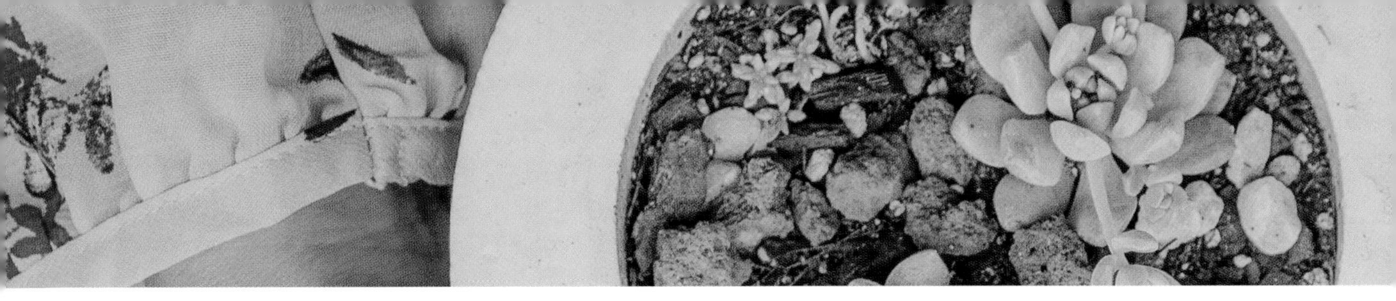

Revelation 2:7). In chapter 12, Solomon again emphasizes that the righteous will bear fruit, and their root will not be moved (Proverbs 12:3, 12). We can compare this to Jesus calling Himself the Vine and His followers the branches (John 15). When we are in Christ, we bear fruit that represents God to the world, and we are secure in Him, the righteous root of David (Isaiah 11:1-2, Revelation 5:5). The Lord can use our lives to lead people to Him so they can experience His presence.

QUESTIONS

Circle the word righteous every time it appears in these chapters. What do you notice by doing this?

What does Proverbs 11:14 teach you about the importance of having accountability with other believers?

Meditate on Proverbs 12:28. How does this verse illustrate the life we have in Jesus Christ?

Proverbs 13-15

In Proverbs 13, we see one of the most helpful pieces of advice regarding our tongues.

When we think carefully about what we say, our tongue can protect our lives (Proverbs 13:3). When we speak carelessly, it can lead to ruin. There is so much power in the words we speak. Jesus gives us His righteousness and shows us how to imitate Him in our speech (Proverbs 13:6, 20). What Solomon says about the teaching of the wise is most certainly true of the teaching of Christ. Jesus's instruction to us is a "fountain of life," and His Words keep us from eternal separation from Him (Proverbs 13:14). His Words, and not ours, hold life. So as we grow in relationship with Him, our words will more and more reflect Christ's sweetness (Colossians 4:6, Ephesians 4:29).

Proverbs 14:2 gives us a clear depiction of those who know the Lord and those who do not. When someone walks in uprightness, they only do so out of a knowledge of who God is. This leads to awe and reverence for who He is. Those who are wicked have blind eyes and hardened hearts to the truth. They do not walk uprightly because instead of loving God, they hate Him. They mock sin, and they do not desire favor with God (Proverbs 14:9). This should drive us to our knees in gratitude and worship of God because there is nothing we could have done in our own sinfulness to fear God. The Lord has allowed us to believe in Him and fear Him, and He has put His Spirit inside of us and given us life (Proverbs 14:27). He has delivered us from death.

We learn in Proverbs 15 that gentleness and peace characterize the people of God, and wrath and anger characterize those who do not know Him (Proverbs 15:1, 18). When our tongues are gentle, Solomon compares them to the tree of life (Proverbs 15:4). The Lord uses gentle tongues to soften the hearts of those who will believe in Jesus! The Lord graciously allows us to be used by Him as He opens eyes and ears to the truth of who He is. Proverbs 15:11 reveals a frightening truth to us—that the Lord sees into the very pits of hell, where unbelievers will dwell for all eternity. This verse reminds us that He is present in all places; He sees everything. We cannot hide any thought, emotion, or word from Him. And while this can cause us to be dismayed in our daily struggle with sin, we can take comfort in knowing that nothing can take away our status as His son or daughter because we are united with Jesus. We can cry out to the Lord, and He will hear and answer us (Proverbs 15:29).

"We can cry out to the Lord, and He will hear and answer us."

QUESTIONS

After reading these chapters, compare and contrast the wise and the righteous with the foolish and the wicked. Why is it important to know the difference?

Reread Proverbs 13:10. How is wisdom related to humility?

Meditate on Proverbs 14:26. What does it mean to find refuge in fearing the Lord?

Proverbs 16-18

At the beginning of Proverbs 16, Solomon makes a series of statements to his son about pleasing and fearing the Lord.

The name that Solomon uses for the Lord in this chapter is "Jehovah." Jehovah means "the existing One" and the "self-existent" or "eternal God." It is important to note that part of being a "self-existent" or "eternal God" is to also be self-sufficient and sovereign over all. Solomon knows that it is easy to focus on ourselves and think we are in charge of our lives, but we are not self-existent or self-sufficient. Only the Lord is sovereign over everything (Proverbs 16:4, 9, 11). And in His sovereign goodness, He has made a way for us to come to know Him. In verse 6, we have a picture of the gospel. The Lord atoned for our sin because of His steadfast love to us, even when we despised His name. Through Christ, we are able to fear God and turn away from sin because He defeated it on the cross (Hebrews 2:14).

In Proverbs 17:9, we also can see a foreshadowing of how Christ will love us. He has covered our offenses because He loves us. Jesus is our greatest and dearest friend, and He has also made a way for us to enter the family of God so that we are co-heirs with Him. He is our divine elder brother who is like us by being human but infinitely above us by also being God (Romans 8:29, Hebrews 2:11). Our elder brother has born our adversity on the cross, and He still continues to intercede for us as we struggle with temptation and sin. This means that He continues to talk to God on our behalf so that we can be presented as righteous before God. Therefore, since we now follow Christ, we set our gaze on Him, our true source of wisdom, and walk step by step in this life, drawing from His strength, graciousness, and love (Proverbs 17:24).

In chapter 17, Solomon reminds us of the power of our speech. We must recognize the power of our tongues to speak life or death or to encourage or wound. Once we realize this power, we realize the need to choose our words wisely (Proverbs 18:21). That said, as much as we can plan, discern, and seek to choose our words wisely, we are still human and can misspeak. Therefore, we take comfort in the truth that the Lord is our refuge, and He can do what we cannot (Proverbs 18:10). We do not find security in righteous living but in the Righteous One. When we live in humility toward

"When we live in humility toward God, we imitate Jesus."

God, we imitate Jesus, the ultimate example of a life poured out for others (Philippians 2:1-11). Christ's humility has exalted Him above all other names, kings, and authorities, and our humility brings more honor to His name.

QUESTIONS

Focus on Proverbs 16:9. Do you tend to over-plan, disregarding the sovereignty of God?

Reread Proverbs 17:28. How does this verse illustrate the importance of choosing words with care?

In what ways does Proverbs 18:1 show you the importance of godly friendships?

Proverbs 19-21

When men and women who claim to not believe in the Lord suffer, they, surprisingly, oftentimes will bring their anger and frustration before God (Proverbs 19:3).

While they have despised and forgotten Him before, suffering causes them to pause and think of Him again. Suffering can be the tool to draw someone to God—it is never purposeless! The Lord's commandments lead to eternal life, but those who despise them and the Lord are headed for eternal death (Proverbs 19:16). When the Lord gives us a new heart and opens our eyes to the truth of the gospel, we begin to properly fear the Lord. We are finally at rest and no longer aimlessly searching for purpose. We are satisfied in God, and no matter what suffering we endure, we know we have Him forever, and that is enough.

Faithfulness is defined as remaining loyal or staying steadfast. Solomon encourages his son to show faithfulness to the Lord and walk in His Ways, but there is only One who is truly faithful and righteous: Jesus Christ (Proverbs 20:6). Jesus is the only one who can claim that He has "kept [His] heart pure" (Proverbs 20:9, Matthew 5:17). He enables us to walk in righteousness and to be cleansed from sin (Proverbs 20:9). When we do, our children and future generations are impacted by the gospel (Proverbs 20:7). And while we try to plan wisely and live to glorify God, we must trust the Lord. The Lord's purpose will always prevail (Proverbs 19:21). He is with us each step of the way, and though we do not always understand His ways, we can trust Him (Proverbs 20:24). He is our steadfast and faithful King. His throne will stand forever (Proverbs 20:28).

"The Lord's purpose will always prevail."

There is nothing that is outside of the Lord's sovereign care. The God who holds the heart of kings in His hand will undoubtedly care for us (Proverbs 21:1). So we can make our plans and live our lives, but we must remember that we should not trust in our plans, rulers, strength, or anything else. Our help and strength come from the Lord alone. He has always been faithful to His people, and He will be faithful to us today in everything we face. The Lord is our source of counsel and wisdom. No human wisdom or counsel can compare to His (Proverbs 21:30). When we look at the world around us, we may be discouraged over the evil and brokenness that we see, but the victory belongs to the Lord (Proverbs 21:31). Jesus will return soon and defeat the enemies of God, and He will reign forever (1 Thessalonians 4:13-18, Revelation 4:8).

QUESTIONS

Meditate on Proverbs 19:11. How does this verse exemplify the character of God?

Reread Proverbs 20:27. What is the Lord's lamp, and why is it good for us?

How does Proverbs 21:2 show you the importance of self-examination and conviction of the Holy Spirit?

Proverbs 22-24

To know and fear the Lord, we must have a proper understanding of who He is and who we are in light of His attributes.

As we know Him more and more, it will drive us to humility, and this humility will allow us to have wisdom. In Proverbs 22, Solomon reminds his son that "wealth, honor, and life" will be given to those who have humility and fear the Lord (Proverbs 22:4). This character description actually points to Jesus. Jesus's life was marked by humility as He emptied Himself of His heavenly status and came to earth in the flesh. He was mocked, scorned, wrongly accused, and crucified, but He overcame death and now sits at the right hand of God (1 Peter 3:22). Jesus has been given all honor, and in Him is eternal life and a beautiful inheritance for those who believe in Him (Ephesians 1).

Solomon also instructs his son to train up his children in fear of the Lord so that they will not depart from the truth as they grow older (Proverbs 22:6). When we look at this verse, we must remember it is not a guarantee or promise to us as we raise our children to know Jesus. Remember, the proverbs do not equate to promises; rather, they offer guidance for living a life that glorifies God. We must trust in the Lord to help us instruct our children about who He is and what He has done through the gospel. Our God is sovereign over the eternal security of our children, and we can trust Him with their lives.

In Proverbs 23, Solomon gives his son a series of "do not" warnings. These statements are straightforward and clear for Solomon's son to follow. Solomon warns his son not to be captivated by power or wealth. He also warns him not to associate with the stingy and foolish. Instead, he implores him to seek wisdom and to carry on Solomon's teaching to his children. Solomon tells his son that it will be his joy to watch him walk in righteousness (Proverbs 23:24). This proverb should bring us hope. If an earthly father experiences joy by watching his children walk in righteousness, we must ask ourselves how much more so will our Heavenly Father rejoice as we follow His ways by patterning our lives after Christ! Let us give our Father our hearts and observe His ways.

"He will make us more like Himself as we abide in Him."

The pursuit of Jesus, who is the embodiment of wisdom, is what keeps us from stumbling. It brings blessing, strength, and knowledge to believers' lives (Proverbs 24:3-5). Following His ways and His Word is like sweet honey for our souls (Proverbs 24:13). Wisdom in Christ gives us hope for our future, and

we will never lose this hope (Proverbs 24:14). Since we still struggle with sin, we will fail in our pursuit of wisdom, but Proverbs 24:16 reminds us that when we fall, we must rely on the Lord's strength and the righteousness we have received in Christ, rise again, and continue to walk in wisdom. The pursuit of wisdom may feel overwhelming as we are made aware of our weakness, but His strength is made perfect in our weakness (2 Corinthians 12:9), and He will make us more like Himself as we abide in Him.

QUESTIONS

Reread Proverbs 22:11. How can you love a pure heart and gracious words?

Meditate on Proverbs 23:17. What are some ways that we tend to envy sinners? Why is this something we should watch out for in our thoughts?

How does Proverbs 24:28-29 remind you of the teaching of Jesus? (Read Matthew 5:38-48 for help!)

Proverbs 25-27

Proverbs 25:1–Proverbs 29:27 make up a collection of Proverbs written by Solomon that were collected about 270 years after his death, during King Hezekiah's reign.

As the collection begins, we see a reminder from Solomon that there are many glorious things that the Lord only knows, but the "glory of kings," or of great men, is to search out the things of God (Proverbs 25:2). We see many passages in Proverbs 25 repeated in the New Testament. Like Solomon, Jesus instructs us not to put ourselves in a position of honor but to walk in humility (Proverbs 25:6-7, Luke 14:8-11). Jesus also tells us to privately confront our neighbor or friend in a dispute (Proverbs 25:9-10, Matthew 18:15). Furthermore, the apostle Paul quotes Proverbs 25:21-22 in Romans 12 when he discusses the marks of a true believer. By noticing that Proverbs is repeated by Jesus and Paul, we can affirm that these verses are still applicable to followers of Jesus and the New Testament is not separate from the Old Testament. Both collections of books tell one unified story.

In Proverbs 26, Solomon warns his son against the ways of the foolish and the lazy. Both of these attributes should not characterize the life of the wise person. However, they do describe some people's lives before they followed Christ. Fools, those who do not know God, refuse to learn wisdom and have to learn through pain (Proverbs 26:3). The slacker avoids work and loves his bed (Proverbs 26:13-14). And, they both are "wise in their own eyes" (Proverbs 26:5).

After warning his son about being "wise in his own eyes," Solomon encourages his son to listen to the gentle rebuke and correction of a friend (Proverbs 27:5-6). He continues to talk about the pleasantness of a friend's advice (Proverbs 27:9). Jesus has called Himself our friend, and in His wisdom, we are sanctified (John 15:15). He gently leads us in the way of righteousness, and He counsels us in each moment of our lives. Though we do not audibly hear Him like we hear a family member or friend, His voice is clear to us in His Word, and His presence is near to us like any other person we see day-to-day. As He disciplines and corrects us, we can trust in our truest and dearest friend.

"As He disciplines and corrects us, we can trust in our truest and dearest friend."

QUESTIONS

What does Proverbs 25:11-12 teach you about godly, wise accountability?

Paraphrase Proverbs 26:23-28 in your own words.

Meditate on verse Proverbs 27:17. How does this verse speak to friendship among Christians?

Proverbs 28-31

When we have received righteousness from Christ, we become "as bold as a lion" (Proverbs 28:1).

"The pursuit of wisdom comes as we fear the Lord."

Our guilt has been removed because of the blood of Christ. He has cleansed us from transgression and given us mercy (Proverbs 28:13, 1 John 1:9). We can face the difficult circumstances of life because He is our strength, and our trust is in Him (Proverbs 28:25-26).

In Proverbs 29, we see a contrast between the righteous and wicked ruler. The world longs for and anticipates its perfectly righteous and just King (Proverbs 29:2). Jesus is the only King who will be completely faithful, and He is also the only King with a throne established forever (Proverbs 29:14). While the authorities and rulers of this world will disappoint us again and again, we are always safe in the hands of our Heavenly King (Proverbs 29:25). He is the only One who will rule with complete justice (Proverbs 29:26).

Proverbs 30 is one of the few proverbs that was not written by Solomon. Instead, it was written by a wise man named Agur. What is striking in his proverb is his humble position before the Lord (Proverbs 30:3-4). Agur challenges us to examine our human limitations and beckons us to marvel at the awesomeness of God. At the end of this description he asks, "Who has established all the ends of the earth? What is his name, and what is the name of his son—if you know?" (Proverbs 30:4). Here we see a direct foreshadowing of Jesus Christ, the Son of God. We know His name!

Proverbs ends just as it began—with the personification of a woman as wisdom. Proverbs 31 conveys the words spoken by the mother of King Lemuel to her son. It is important to note that this is the only time in the Scriptures that King Lemuel is mentioned and that scholars disagree on who Lemuel actually was. One thing we do know is that Lemuel was one of God's people as his name means "belonging to God." Regardless of Lemuel's identity, we know that Proverbs 31 is Lemuel's mother's description of a good wife. It is incredibly important to note that Proverbs 31 is neither a checklist for women, nor is it a to-do list to work through. Instead, Proverbs 31 is the description of the character of a woman who seeks the Lord. We have no reason to be intimidated by all that this woman does. Instead, we can be encouraged because of God's power in us. We cannot mimic this woman of wisdom in

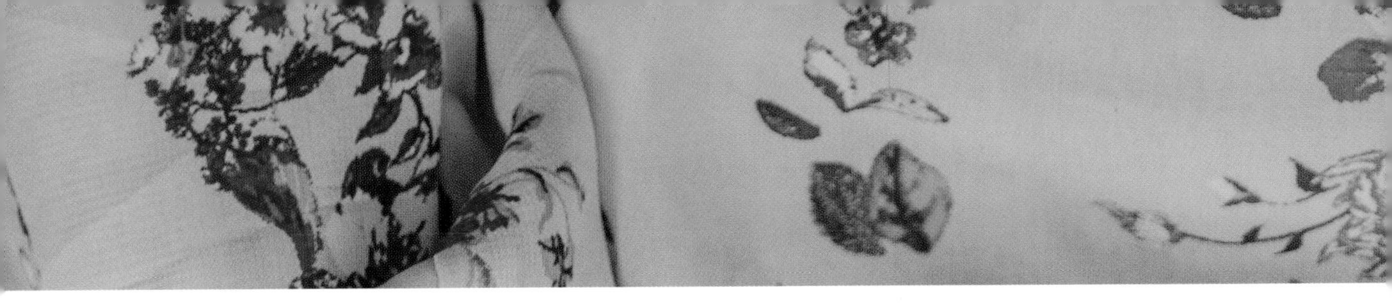

our strength, but He can give us the wisdom to demonstrate her strength of character in our own unique circumstances and lives. This is the same lesson stated throughout Proverbs as we are reminded that the pursuit of wisdom comes as we fear the Lord.

QUESTIONS

How does Proverbs 29:8 teach you about the importance of gentle, kind, exhorting language?

How does knowing that Proverbs 31 is not a checklist for womanhood change the way that you understand the chapter?

Now that we have finished reading through the book of Proverbs, reflect on some of the most important things that the Lord taught you.

Fear God and keep His commands.

Ecclesiastes

GENRE: *Wisdom, Poetry*

AUTHOR / DATE WRITTEN

Unknown, likely Solomon • c. 935-930 BC

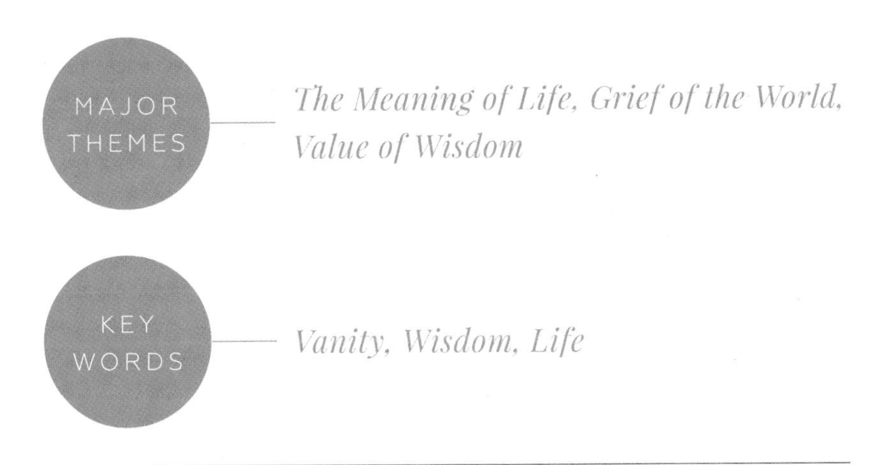

KEY VERSE

ECCLESIASTES 12:13

When all has been heard, the conclusion of the matter is this: fear God and keep his commands, because this is for all humanity.

Ecclesiastes 1-3

While the author of the book of Ecclesiastes is technically unknown, many commentators and biblical scholars believe that King Solomon wrote it.

"The things and people of this earth are temporary, but what God does endures forever."

Regardless of whether he wrote it, Solomon and his quest to discover life's purpose are the book's subjects. As such, we will refer to the author as Solomon as we study the following chapters. The author's primary goal in Ecclesiastes is to confront us with the meaninglessness of life apart from God. All the pursuits of man pass away and lead to nothing in the end, but everything changes when we are in Christ.

As the author opens the book, he uses a phrase we will see repeated throughout Ecclesiastes: "Absolute futility. Everything is futile" (Ecclesiastes 1:2). Generation after generation of people are here and then gone, and the earth keeps going on and on. The sun rises and sets day after day, and streams always run to the sea but never completely fill it. When we do not look at nature and recognize God's glorious handiwork, man will only see the weariness in creation. This represents the weariness man faces in life without God. He toils for nothing because nothing he gains can provide anything of eternal value for him. But because of Jesus, we do not have to labor in vain, and our hope is not in this world that is passing away, but in our eternal home (1 Corinthians 15:58, Philippians 3:20).

Solomon indulged himself in all of the pleasures the world offered and still concluded that it was all "futile" (Ecclesiastes 2:11-12). He was one of the wisest men who ever lived, and yet he considered wisdom futile as well. This is because the more understanding a person has, the more sorrow will naturally follow because they understand the purposelessness of man's toils (Ecclesiastes 1:18). In contrast, Jesus teaches us not to indulge ourselves but to serve and love others. He saved us from only chasing after meaningless pursuits and gave us a life of abundance in Him (John 10:10). And while Solomon walked the earth before Christ, He foreshadows a life of abundance in Jesus. He calls readers to see all of their enjoyment as coming from the hand of God, and to the one who is pleasing to Him, God gives "wisdom, knowledge, and joy" (Ecclesiastes 2:26).

In chapter 3, the writer tells us that there is a time and season for everything, and though we do not always understand why certain things come to pass, we can trust that God has appointed every single season of life. He makes all things beautiful, and He has put a desire for Himself into the heart of every man and woman (Ecclesiastes 3:11). The one thing that unites all people, regardless of their wealth or social status, is death. Everyone we know today, both the humble and famous, will one day breath their last, return to the dust, and be forgotten (Ecclesiastes 3:20). While dwelling on this could certainly depress us, we need to see Solomon's message in light of the gospel. The things and people of this earth are temporary, but what God does endures forever (Ecclesiastes 3:14). People may forget our name, but we are fully known by the Lord when we are in Jesus. Death is the doorway we enter to eternal life with Him.

QUESTIONS

Read 1 Kings 3:5-14. How does this passage help give you a foundation for understanding Solomon's writing in Ecclesiastes?

What does Ecclesiastes 2 teach you about what truly satisfies us? Is our satisfaction found in the world or in God?

Meditate on Ecclesiastes 3:14. What does this teach you about God's character? How can this comfort and encourage you today?

Ecclesiastes 4-6

Solomon gives us a bit of hope at the end of chapter 3, but as chapter 4 opens, he again focuses on the despair in life.

"When we rely on our wealth instead of on the Lord, we miss having true joy from our dependence on Him.

He mourns the life of the oppressed who have no one to comfort them while they labor on earth under terrible conditions for wicked men (Ecclesiastes 4:1). Solomon thinks that it is better not to be alive than to face life's meaninglessness. It is even more terrible to face the futility of toil when your labor is also forced and oppressive! When Jesus begins His earthly ministry, He says that He fulfills the promise of a coming Messiah. This is also referred to as the Messianic promise, which is described in Isaiah 61:1: "The Spirit of the Lord God is on me because the Lord has anointed me to bring good news to the poor. He has sent me to heal the brokenhearted, to proclaim liberty to the captives and freedom to the prisoners."

While Jesus did not cease all oppression from wreaking havoc on the earth, He does offer spiritual freedom and healing to all people. Even if we are oppressed and wrongly treated, we can take comfort that our souls are free from sin and we have a beautiful inheritance in Christ! Solomon also encourages us to not labor alone but with companions (Ecclesiastes 4:9-12). This reminds us of the importance of remaining faithful to the church, the body of Christ. We need one another as we face the harsh realities of this world and prepare for the next.

When we do not come before the Lord and listen to Him, we can become consumed with the things of this world that do not have eternal value. But when we draw near to God, we need to remember who He is and have humility before Him. Solomon tells us to remember, "God is in heaven and you are on earth, so let your words be few" (Ecclesiastes 5:2). He then continues to emphasize the futility of wealth. For some wealthy people, their possessions consume them and give their owner more to worry about, but no one can take any possessions in death (Ecclesiastes 5:11-12, 15). Jesus also warns us against the love of money and encourages us to lay up treasures in the kingdom of heaven (Matthew 6:19-24). What we do for the kingdom of heaven today lasts forever. Jesus does not mean that it is wrong to be wealthy, but when we rely on our wealth instead of on the Lord, we miss having true joy from our dependence on Him. This life passes away quickly, and we need to live our lives in preparation for His physical, eternal kingdom (Ecclesiastes 6:12-13).

QUESTIONS

What does it mean in Ecclesiastes 4:12 that a cord of three strands is not easily broken?

Read 1 Peter 1:7 and Ecclesiastes 5:10. How do these verses convey to you the things we should find valuable?

Paraphrase chapter 6 in your own words.

Ecclesiastes 7-9

As we begin reading chapter 7, the style and language of Ecclesiastes remind us of the wisdom of Proverbs.

"The fear of God will always surpass the wisdom and strength the world offers."

Here, Solomon again contrasts wisdom and folly. He tells us what is "better," and some of his answers are surprising. He says that the day someone dies is better than the day that person is born (Ecclesiastes 7:1). In light of Solomon's musings on the meaninglessness and futility of life, this fits his previous thoughts. As believers in Jesus, Ecclesiastes 7:1 is true in that the day we die is not sorrowful but is a beautiful gain (Philippians 1:21)! Death brings us into the presence of Jesus. Solomon also encourages his readers to go into the "house of mourning" instead of "a house of feasting" (Ecclesiastes 7:2). As morbid as it may sound, our eventual destination will be in a casket in the house of mourning, but if you have ever witnessed the funeral service of a person who deeply loved Christ, there is immense hope and joy in the celebration of his or her life. Solomon's words emphasize the importance of living for eternity and not just for the here and now. It is good to remember that our lives are fleeting (James 4:14).

However, just because our lives are quickly passing away does not mean we forsake living in wisdom. Solomon thus encourages his readers to obey the king or their earthly authorities (Ecclesiastes 8:2). By doing so, we show that we fear God because God has sovereignly allowed that person to have authority. Solomon laments that those who are wicked are often not punished for their wickedness in this life. It makes the pursuit of righteousness seem insignificant, but Solomon ultimately knows that it will go well with those who fear the Lord (Ecclesiastes 8:12-13). Sometimes we are tempted to question God's ways, especially when it seems that righteous people often suffer and the wicked live lives of ease. The wicked may seem to prosper if you are only looking at the present day, but we are not simply living for the present; we live for our future hope in Jesus. Solomon tells us that living in wisdom means that we focus on the eternal. Jesus preached this same message at the Sermon on the Mount in Matthew 5 as He called us to look forward to the kingdom of Heaven.

All of us will reach the end of our lives and meet the same fate. Ultimately, your social or economic status does not matter. Everyone dies. So Solomon encourages us to enjoy our lives with people who we love, to work hard with

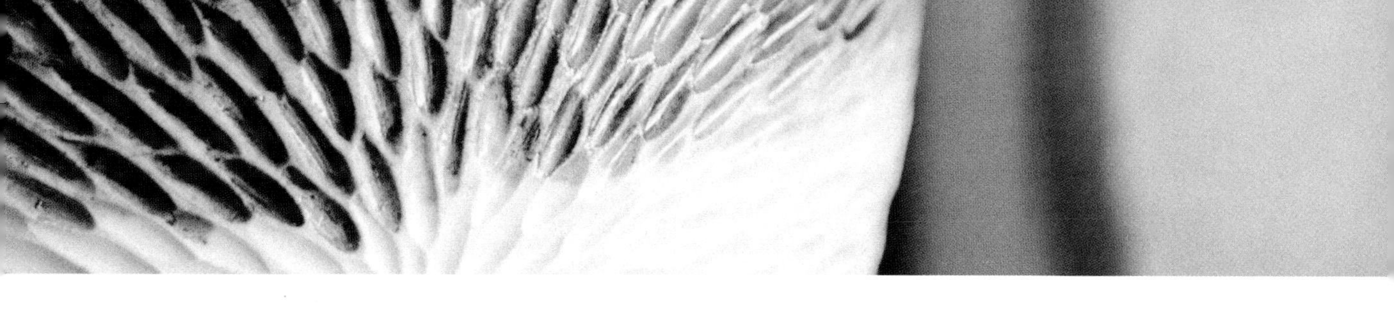

our hands, and to use our time well (Ecclesiastes 9:7-10). Time takes its toll on everyone, regardless of strength and ability. And while everyone will meet death, it is still good to consider how to live wisely in the present. Solomon tells us that wisdom overcomes the mightiest of armies and rulers, which shows us that the fear of God will always surpass the wisdom and strength the world offers (Ecclesiastes 9:15-18). As we draw near to Jesus and His life-giving Word, we will understand how to live in a manner worthy of Him until our time on earth comes to a close.

QUESTIONS

So far in the book of Ecclesiastes, what do you think King Solomon is trying to convey to his audience?

Reread Ecclesiastes 8:8-9. What does this passage teach you about the wisdom and authority of the Lord?

Spend some time in prayer, thanking the Lord that we have hope in His Son and asking that He would give you wisdom.

Ecclesiastes 10-12

Solomon concludes his thoughts on how it is good to live in wisdom, and he tells us in Ecclesiastes 10 why we need to avoid walking in foolishness.

"We can rest in what Jesus has done and who He is to bring purpose and joy to this life."

Ecclesiastes 10:1 gives us a grave warning about the effect of folly on our lives. We can have wisdom and honor, but it will all be ruined if we give in to certain foolish mistakes. Solomon compares it to dead flies found in expensive perfume. However, sometimes, the lives of the foolish are publicly commended and not rebuked, which reminds us that this world loves darkness instead of light (John 3:19). While the world's foolishness and wickedness may be elevated above righteousness, there is a day that is coming when all will be made right, and the wisdom of the world will bow before Christ. Regardless of how it may appear, foolishness has an exhausting and burdensome effect on a person's soul (Ecclesiastes 10:8-20). As we interact with people who do not know God and are bound to foolishness, let us show them the freedom and rest that is found in following Jesus and knowing His wisdom (Matthew 11:28-30).

In Ecclesiastes 11, Solomon gives his final advice on living in a world where everything seems meaningless. It could be easy to become caught up in the unknowns of life, but ultimately we can trust in the Lord and what He has ordained for us (Ecclesiastes 11:5). Our lives are short and passing away, but this should not keep us from being faithful with the life we have been given. We remember that our youth will not last forever, but growing old with the Lord is our joy as we can know Him more and anticipate being in His presence. We continually seek to use our lives for the glory of Christ and His kingdom as we live in this world.

In Ecclesiastes, Solomon examined whether life was worth living, and at first glance, his answer was "no." But then he looked at life again and concluded that it is worth living if we have the Lord (Ecclesiastes 12:13-14). Life without God is meaningless and full of suffering and uncertainty, but Jesus brings purpose to this life. In fact, He even brings purpose to our pain. This life is an adventure and a gift, and God desires for us to enjoy it and steward it well. Instead of living this life consumed by worry and fear, we can find safety and counsel in the fear of the Lord. In fearing the Lord, we find reverence for His purposes, and we find meaning for this life in such a

way that our early fears are diminished. As believers, we do not need to fear anything else, even death. We can rest in what Jesus has done and who He is to bring purpose and joy to this life. Solomon gives great wisdom, but ultimately he points us to Jesus, our Shepherd King, who is God's embodied wisdom (Matthew 12:42). As we abide in Christ, we can look to Him for wisdom moment by moment, and we are at peace with the brevity of our life rather than fearful of it. Our Savior will be with us until the very end, and then we will be with Him forever.

QUESTIONS

Meditate on Ecclesiastes 10:1-4. How does this encourage you to flee from folly? What effect can folly have on your life?

Reread Ecclesiastes 11:5. How does this verse illustrate the wonders of God's craftsmanship?

Focus on Ecclesiastes 12:14. What does this verse show you about the character of God?

Love is
as strong
as death.

Song of Solomon

GENRE: *Wisdom, Poetry*

AUTHOR / DATE WRITTEN

Possibly King Solomon • c. 965 BC

KEY VERSES

SONG OF SOLOMON 8:6-7

Set me as a seal on your heart, as a seal on your arm. For love is as strong as death; jealousy is as unrelenting as Sheol. Love's flames are fiery flames—an almighty flame! A huge torrent cannot extinguish love; rivers cannot sweep it away. If a man were to give all his wealth for love, it would be utterly scorned.

Song of Solomon 1-4

The Song of Solomon, or the Song of Songs, is another book written either by Solomon or in his honor during his reign.

The book highlights the beauty and joy of marriage, which is a picture of God's love for His people and represents the relationship between Christ and His church. While the Song of Solomon reminds us of God's love for His people, we must be careful not to look at this account as only an allegory. The book points us to Jesus and His love for His church, but its primary purpose is to show us how God has created both love and sexuality as gifts to be enjoyed in marriage.

The first chapters of Song of Solomon set forth the excitement and beauty that is in marriage, love, and sex when done God's way. As the bride speaks of her husband, she says that his "love is better than wine" (Song of Solomon 1:2 ESV). She desires for him to take her into his chambers so that they can physically declare their love for one another. The bride deeply desires her husband, and he desires her. As we pursue Christ and know Him more and more, we will begin to see that His love is truly better than wine as well. In fact, it is better than anything we could ever experience, and He gives it freely to us! We deeply desire and treasure Him as we understand His love. And just as the groom brings the bride to the banqueting house and puts a "banner of love" over her, so Christ puts His love on us (Romans 5:5).

The groom's invitation to the bride to "come" in Song of Solomon 2:10-12 reminds us of Jesus's invitation to all as seen throughout God's Word (Matthew 11:28-30, Isaiah 1:18, Luke 14:17, Revelation 22:17). And when we accept Jesus's invitation to follow Him, the winter of our hearts being spiritually dead is over. It is truly a time for singing. Though earthly marriage can provide joy and companionship, it is God alone who can satisfy the longing in our hearts. God's design for marriage is that the relationship would point to Him. The world we live in today has taken sex and marred it for sinful and selfish purposes, but the author of Song of Solomon warns us to not awaken this gift of marital love until its proper time (Song of Solomon 3:5). When believers of Christ display the enjoyment of marriage, sex, and love the way God intended, He is glorified.

"When we accept Jesus's invitation to follow Him, the winter of our hearts being spiritually dead is over."

QUESTIONS

In what ways do these chapters point you to Christ?

Read Revelation 22:17. How can you see the content of the Song of Solomon reflected in this verse?

Why will earthly love never satisfy us like the love of God?

Song of Solomon 5-8

The Song of Solomon is unlike any other book in the Bible. It shows us the beauty, joy, and pleasure that God has designed for marriage.

Throughout this book, the bride and groom delight in their romance and love, and they constantly desire to be with each other. They each find joy, pleasure, and satisfaction in their spouse. Their marriage is an example of godly marriages—full of life, love, adoration, and steadfastness. However, more than that, we also see how their marriage mirrors our relationship with Christ.

Song of Solomon 5 is an example of how a godly marriage mirrors our relationship with Christ. In this chapter, the bride dreams of her husband and longs to be with him, just as we long to be reunited with Christ. While we know He has promised to always be with us, we desire to see His face and be physically present with Him in His eternal kingdom (Matthew 28:20, Philippians 1:23). The bride and groom speak of delighting in each other in a lush, bountiful garden which makes us think of the garden of Eden and how God ordained the first marriage between Adam and Eve (Song of Solomon 6:2-3, 11-12, 7:11-13). The bride and groom's marriage mirrors our relationship with God, which was the primary purpose of marriage when God created it in the garden of Eden. Our God delights and loves us. He has entered a covenant with us, and we find our joy in Him. He has pursued and won our hearts through the gospel, and now we pursue Him. His love for us is unending and greater than anything this world has to offer.

The bride's poem about love closes the Song of Solomon and reminds us of the strength of the Lord's love for us, which God showed through Jesus's death on the cross (Song of Solomon 8:6-7). Truly, the Lord's love is "as strong as death" as He came in the person of Jesus Christ to die for the sins of His people (Song of Solomon 8:6, John 3:16). And once we are in Christ, nothing can ever separate us from the love of God (Romans 8:38-39).

The book of Song of Solomon is primarily a love poem between a husband and wife, but it also shows us the riches of the love between the Lord and us, as marriage is derived from Him and reflects who He is. As we participate in marriage or encourage our friends in their marriages, we must remember that these relationships display the love of God to a watching world. God's love is meant to be deeply enjoyed, just like the love between a husband and wife, so we must safeguard the intimacy of marriage to honor the Lord and His holy, consuming love.

"God's love is meant to be deeply enjoyed."

QUESTIONS

In what ways does Song of Solomon remind you of the covenant love that we have with God?

How is the love of God superior to any earthly love?

What are some of the most prominent things God has taught you from reading the Song of Solomon?

The Lord
is a
just God.

Isaiah

GENRE: *Prophet, Pre-exilic*

AUTHOR / DATE WRITTEN

Isaiah • c. 739-631 BC

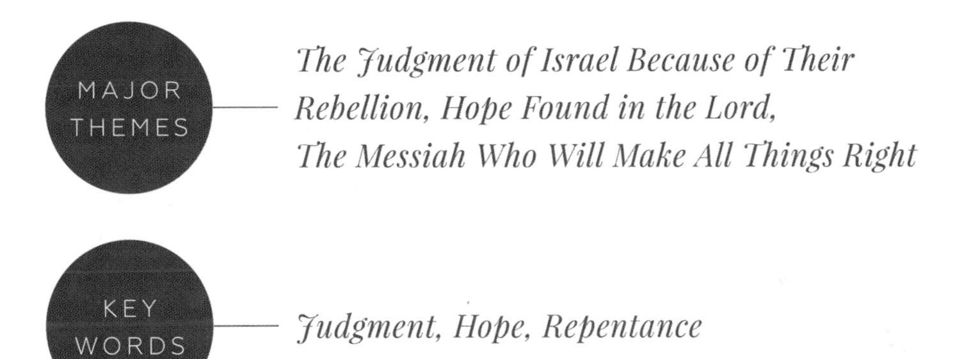

KEY VERSE

ISAIAH 30:18

Therefore the Lord is waiting to show you mercy, and is rising up to show you compassion, for the Lord is a just God. All who wait patiently for him are happy.

Isaiah 1-3

The name "Isaiah" means "salvation is of the Lord," and as the Lord warns His people of coming judgment through the prophet Isaiah, He will fulfill the prophet's name and remind them again and again that He is their salvation.

Isaiah begins with God speaking to the prophet in a vision. At the time Isaiah prophesied, the nation of Israel was already split into two kingdoms: Israel and Judah. Israel was already being conquered by Assyria and was ruled by wicked kings. Therefore, most of Isaiah's prophecies are about Judah, who had good and wicked rulers and was prone to disobey God.

Judah had rejected and rebelled, and yet the Lord still longed to call them back to Himself. His steadfast love was so much stronger than their sin. Though the record of their sin had declared them guilty, the Lord was ready and waiting to offer full pardon. And, He will do the same for us. He takes away our guilt and makes us white as snow by washing us in the blood of Jesus (Isaiah 1:18, 1 John 1:7-9). And even when He comes with the sobering truth that sin has consequences, He brings the promise of redemption. He redeems everything. He takes away our weakness and brokenness and uses it to show us His extravagant love and mercy. Though we rebel and reject Him, He stands with arms open wide, ready and waiting to redeem and restore. He is truth and justice perfectly coupled with love and grace. He will redeem.

"Nothing that God does is separate from His lovingkindness and steadfast love."

In chapter 2, Isaiah gives a promise full of future hope as he describes the future city of God, which will draw people from all nations (Isaiah 2:1-4). As believers, we are among the nations the Lord has drawn to Himself through Christ. And someday, we will run with believers from every nation to the courts of our God, and we will finally be with Him again. There will be no more violence and death, but only the Lord's peace and light, and we will walk in it for all of our days (Isaiah 2:5). The people of Judah were not living in a way to point the nations to this future kingdom. They were living like all of the other nations of the world, so the Lord promised them a day where He would act against them to humble them (Isaiah 2:12). Judah had become just like Sodom and Gomorrah, proudly living in sin and oppressing the poor, and God would not have this for His people (Isaiah 1:9-10, 3:8-9, 3:13-15). And while the judgment of the Lord would be upon His people, He would protect and uphold a faithful remnant, and the Messiah would still come from the line of Judah (Isaiah 3:10). It may be difficult to read about the judgment of God, but nothing that God does is separate from His lovingkindness and steadfast love. God is full of wrath toward sin because it opposes Him and hurts His creation. He disciplines us to make us into His likeness and to rid us of sin. The process may be painful, but it is always for our good and His glory. There is freedom as we surrender our sin and walk in the way of Jesus.

QUESTIONS

What does God reveal about His character when He sends a vision to His people through Isaiah? What does this action tell us about who He is?

Reread Isaiah 1:4. How does this verse give you a foundational understanding of the purpose of God's message to Israel?

We see God called "The Lord God of Hosts" or "armies" multiple times in this reading. What do you think that this is trying to communicate to the reader?

Isaiah 4-6

The people of God had drifted far from the Lord, but God brought hope to their desperate situation.

“He is our hope, and He will be with us.”

In chapter 4, we are introduced to the “Branch of the Lord,” which is another name for Jesus. How amazing that as Judah hears their judgment from God, He also emphasizes their future hope in the promised Messiah. After they undergo judgment, there will be a faithful remnant who will return to Jerusalem. The text also uses the name “Zion” for Jerusalem, which is also a reference to the city of God in eternity. Those who belong to this city will be called holy, and God will cleanse them from sin. God says that His presence in Zion will be like the pillar of fire and the cloud that the people of Israel experienced as they left Egypt (Isaiah 4:5). He will know His people intimately in this heavenly city, and this is a city to which all believers of Jesus belong. We have hope for this future day as well!

Chapter 5 shows how far Israel had drifted from God as Isaiah tells the parable of the Lord and His vineyard, where He has planted Israel as His vine, but they had not produced good fruit (Isaiah 5:1-7). The Lord had constantly been faithful though the people had been quick to wander from Him. The parable of the vineyard reminds us of John 15 when Jesus declares Himself the “true vine” of His Father’s vineyard (John 15:1). Jesus is the greater Israel who walks in perfect righteousness and obeys the Lord. By remaining in Christ, our sustaining vine, we are given the righteousness of Christ, and we bear good fruit.

Throughout the book of Isaiah, we see the contrast between people who wander and rebel and a faithful, loving God who pursues them anyway. We identify with them as we also wander from the Lord and choose our sin over obedience to Him. The reality of their unfaithfulness, as well as our own unfaithfulness, is disheartening, but Isaiah shows that the Lord’s love is stronger.

In chapter 6, Isaiah has a vision of the Lord on His throne in heaven. When Isaiah saw God’s glory, He was humbled and aware of His own weakness and sin. However, Isaiah was not left without hope, and neither are we. The holy God of all stands with arms outstretched, ready to redeem the most broken parts of us for His glory. He will not fail us or ever let us down. He will be there when we call His name. He will show us Himself and never leave us hopeless or alone. He is our hope, and He will be with us.

QUESTIONS

What does Isaiah chapter 4 teach us about God's faithfulness?

Read John 15:1-16. How does this passage further your understanding of the imagery of the vineyard in Isaiah 5?

How does Isaiah 6:5-7 speak to the grace, mercy, and kindness of God? How have we experienced something similar to Isaiah through the death, burial, and resurrection of Jesus Christ?

Isaiah 7-9

During the writing of Isaiah, the kingdom was divided with Israel in the north and Judah in the south.

"The Messiah will make the darkness light and lift the burden the people carried."

These chapters reflect the time of turmoil surrounding God's people. Judah saw imminent destruction coming from the hand of Assyria and Ephraim—Ephraim is another name for Israel's northern kingdom. Judah's kinsmen were coming against them, and the king of Judah, Ahaz, was fearful. He looked for help from the hands of Assyria, the very people who would later bring destruction to Israel. And yet, amid wars and uncertainty came the promise of a Messiah. Isaiah 7:14 speaks of Immanuel, born of a virgin. This promise's final fulfillment is made clear in Matthew 1:18-25 when Jesus comes as our Immanuel. It is important to note here that Immanuel means "God with us." God's promise to Judah as they see their enemies closing in on them was that He was with them, and this promise is ultimately carried out in the incarnation of Christ.

The Lord describes the Assyrian invasion more in chapter 8, but He tenderly reminds Isaiah to trust in Him. He prepares Isaiah for how the people will react to the judgment of God. They will be full of fear and dread, but Isaiah and the faithful remnant should not fear or dread, for they know the Lord. And His holiness is much more to be feared and dreaded than the Assyrians. To fear the Lord is to be in awe of His perfect holiness—to stand in awe and reverence of His power, glory, and majesty. Isaiah instructs those who are faithful to God in Judah to wait upon Him and put their hope in Him. While those in Judah who have rejected the Lord will try to find comfort and answers from anywhere but the Lord, Isaiah is told to not listen to their demands or be overcome by their anguish, for their hope is not in the Lord.

In this seemingly hopeless moment in Judah's history, another promise of the coming Messiah is given. Despite their sin, redemption and restoration are promised. The Messiah will make the darkness light and lift the burden the people carried. He will be their "Wonderful Counselor, Mighty God, Eternal Father, Prince of Peace" (Isaiah 9:6). He would be everything that they needed. He would bring peace between God and man and peace in the hearts of all those who followed Him. War and destruction will not be forever.

QUESTIONS

Read Isaiah 7:14 and Matthew 1:18-25 together. Meditate on the amount of time that passed between the prophecy and the birth of Jesus. What does this show us about God? How can this be an encouragement to you?

How does the promise of a Messiah in Isaiah 7:14 bring hope in the surrounding chapter?

What does Isaiah 9 teach you about the Lord's anger? Is it ever unprovoked? Do you see the Lord's long-suffering in this chapter?

Isaiah 10-12

It was a turbulent time for God's people, but He never forgets His promises.

"What He has done should fill our hearts with overwhelming gratitude and praise."

In the midst of prophecies of judgment, God promises that a remnant of His people will return from exile. God promises this because of His covenant with Abraham (Genesis 12:2-3, Deuteronomy 7:7-10, Psalm 105:8-11). God will do what He said He would do. While the king of Assyria may boast and proclaim his might over them, he was only a tool in the Lord's hands to carry out His sovereign plan (Isaiah 10:12-15). Just like the Lord brought Egypt to ruin, so would be the fate of Assyria. As the people of Judah are taken captive by the Assyrians, they could rest in knowing that justice would one day come by the hand of the Lord, even though they could not see it yet. This faithful remnant would be spared!

Chapter 11 shows again how God will keep His promises in the coming of the Messiah. Jesus is the fulfillment of this promise, and He would fulfill every word of it. Jesus is the Righteous Branch from the line of Jesse. He will allow those who call on His name to bear good fruit. When Jesus begins His ministry and is baptized by John the Baptist, the Holy Spirit descends upon Him and fulfills the words, "The Spirit of the Lord will rest on Him" (Isaiah 11:2, Luke 3:22). Jesus walked in understanding and fear of God. After he dies on the cross and is resurrected, He creates a new humanity that brings God's peace and love to a world in chaos. Much of the promise in Isaiah 11 would be fulfilled in Christ's first coming, but some of the promises will see their full completion in His second coming. Someday, when Christ's physical kingdom comes to earth, there will be peace forever. The world will be free from the curse of sin (I Corinthians 15:50-58).

Chapter 12 presents the response God's people will have on that day and the attitude our hearts should have even now. What He has done should fill our hearts with overwhelming gratitude and praise for all He has done and who He is. While the people of Judah will be tempted to question and reject God for His judgment, He has promised that they will see Him as their salvation. There is a day coming when the world will finally bow to God as Creator, and His people will be with Him forever.

QUESTIONS

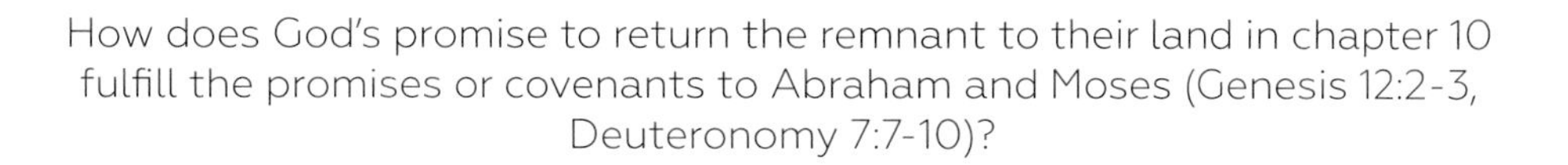

How does God's promise to return the remnant to their land in chapter 10 fulfill the promises or covenants to Abraham and Moses (Genesis 12:2-3, Deuteronomy 7:7-10)?

In what ways does chapter 11 point toward Jesus Christ?

Paraphrase the song in chapter 12.

Isaiah 13-15

In chapter 13, Isaiah begins a series of prophetic judgments to the nations that will go on until chapter 23.

While the Lord began the book of Isaiah by declaring His judgment on His people for their sin, He now turns to speak to Babylon, the people who will carry Judah into exile. This prophecy was given many years before Babylon was even a world power. Throughout the Bible, Babylon will represent the kingdoms of the world who are opposed to God. The Lord will have His day of wrath against the Babylonians, but there is also a day coming where He will have judgment over all of the earth (Isaiah 13:9-11). This passage points forward to that day when Christ returns (Isaiah 13:10, Matthew 24:29). When Jesus comes back to the earth to reign, He will bring justice against those who have opposed God, and He will deliver His people from the curse of sin forever.

After the Lord finishes His promise of judgment for Babylon, He promises hope and deliverance for Judah. He will have compassion on them and bring them home (Isaiah 14:1). Not only that, but Israel will have victory over their captors, and they will sing a song of triumph over them. Babylon had once defeated Israel, but now God will humble them. Later in chapter 14, we are given a description of Babylon's king, who has fallen after trying to place himself in equal standing with the Lord (Isaiah 14:12-16). The King James Version of the Bible translates this king's description of the "shining morning star" as "Lucifer." Lucifer is another name for Satan. While many wicked kings have ruled and still rule over the earth, they are always only representatives of the ultimate enemy of God, Satan. Satan is the king of Babylon, which is to say, he is the king of the world who opposes God. From the beginning of Satan's corruption, he has tried to esteem himself to be like God, but he never will achieve this. God is unparalleled, and Satan has a final destiny that is already written. He will burn in a lake of fire forever (Revelation 20:10). Followers of Jesus will one day sing a song of triumph when Satan is defeated and sin and death are no more (Revelation 19:3). We will be able to finally follow the Lord wholeheartedly and be free from the oppression of the enemy of God.

Isaiah 15 contains the Lord's judgment against the nation of Moab. Moab was the hometown of Ruth, making them also part of the lineage of David and Jesus. As we read the judgment of Moab, we notice a unique empathy from the

"He will always do what is just and right."

Lord that was not evident in the judgment of Babylon (Isaiah 15:5). The Moabites were actually distantly related to the Israelites since they descended from the incestual relationship between Lot and one of his daughters after she made Lot drunk and slept with him (Genesis 19:30-38). God does not delight in having to punish sin, but He disciplines for the good of His creation. He will always do what is just and right. He will not let evil flourish forever, and until the day that evil is removed from this earth, He will be a refuge for His people.

QUESTIONS

What does Isaiah 13 show you about God's character?

Reread Isaiah 14:1-2. How do these verses teach you about God's generosity? How can this give you hope today?

Spend some time in self-examination. Do you tend to overlook God's justice? How do these chapters help you to better understand God's justice?

Isaiah 16-18

It was a turbulent time for God's people, but He never forgets His promises.

The prophetic judgments against Moab continue in Isaiah 16. Isaiah prophesies that though the Moabites were once an enemy of God's people, they looked to Judah for help when trouble came. The Lord instructed His people to let the outcasts of Moab sojourn among them. They were to give them shelter and safety from those who were trying to destroy them (Isaiah 16:4). The Messiah King, who we know will be Jesus, is promised again in this passage. He is contrasted with Moab and the nations who seek only to oppress and destroy. His reign will be characterized by steadfast love and faithfulness (Isaiah 16:5).

God continues to pronounce judgment, but now on Damascus (located in Syria) and Israel, who have joined forces against Judah. Israel, the northern kingdom of God's chosen people, had formed an alliance with a foreign nation against their brothers. The Lord's judgment will ultimately lead the people of these nations to recognize God for who He is and worship Him as their Lord. Idols and man-made gods will no longer matter because they could not deliver the people of Syria and Israel from the day of the Lord (Isaiah 17:7-8). These verses remind us to focus our hearts on the Lord alone instead of being distracted by worldly things. There is nothing this world has to offer that is more precious than the Lord. There is nothing that even compares. May our hearts yearn for the Giver, and not just the gifts.

In Isaiah 18, God tells Judah to send messengers to the people of Cush—the Ethiopians. The Cushites had sent ambassadors to Judah before, but now the people of God would go to them. The Lord was making a way for the Cushites to worship and know Him. Here is a beautiful revelation: God will use His people's exile and deliverance to draw the nations to Himself. Assyria and Babylon will be humbled, and the world will watch and see the hand of the one true God. Jesus continues this mission to make God known among the world when He sends His disciples into the whole world to preach the gospel (Matthew 28:16-20). Jesus's kingdom is for every tribe, tongue, and nation.

"There is nothing this world has to offer that is more precious than the Lord."

QUESTIONS

Meditate on Isaiah 16:5. To whom do you think this is referring?

After reading about Moab, what are some ways that you are prone to the same actions?

Spend some time in prayer while dwelling on Isaiah 17:10. Ask that God would always remind you of who He is. Ask for strength to obey and love Him.

Isaiah 19-21

In chapter 19, Egypt receives a prophecy of judgment from the Lord.

Egypt was one of the most powerful nations in the ancient world, and they are mentioned all the way back in the book of Genesis. Egypt, like Babylon, became a representative for all the enemies of God and His people. Egypt was the perfect example of man's wisdom, as they thought they were undefeatable, but the world's wisdom is foolish compared to God's wisdom (Isaiah 19:11-13). True strength and wisdom are found in the Lord alone.

But there is hope, even for Egypt. Egypt would someday turn to the Lord. The nation that had gone against God in pride and had oppressed God's people would be delivered from their oppressors by the Lord Himself. He would send them a Savior who would even live among them (Isaiah 19:20, Matthew 2:13-15). God would extend mercy, and after the beginning of the early church, there would be a strong Christian presence in Egypt for nearly 600 years. God promises deliverance for Assyria as well, the nation that will destroy the northern kingdom of Israel. In His goodness and providence, God uses judgment to restore His chosen remnant of people to Himself, and He brings people from all nations into His family. Israel is the conduit to display the Lord's glory to the world. The deliverance of Egypt and Assyria reminds us that we have also been brought into the family of God by His mercy and grace (Ephesians 1:5). The gospel of Jesus delivers us from the domain of darkness and into His kingdom (Colossians 1:13).

"People opposed to God desperately need to hear the gospel."

In Chapter 20, we see the kingdom of Assyria threaten Judah, and as a result, they turn to the nations of Egypt and Cush for help. They look for aid from the world instead of pleading to God to deliver them. To show them their foolishness, the Lord instructs Isaiah to do the unthinkable. He will walk around completely naked for three years to show how Egypt and Cush, Judah's supposedly mighty allies, would be conquered and treated by Assyria (Isaiah 20:3-6). All of the exiles from these nations would be naked like Isaiah as they left their homes. The Lord wanted Judah to rely on Him and not Egypt and Cush. When we look to man to save us, we forget we have access to the strength of Jesus. When we are saved, we are united with Him (John 15). The help the world offers is nothing compared to the wisdom, strength, and deliverance we have in Christ.

Isaiah then declares the Lord's judgment of Babylon. The Persian empire will eventually destroy Babylon—the nation that carried Judah in exile. Babylon

will eat, drink, and feast as the Persians and Medes lay siege to the city. The Babylonians thought their city was impenetrable, but they will be conquered and slaughtered (Daniel 5). When we remember that Babylon represents all the world's kingdoms and people who are opposed to God, we see that this chapter also describes the future judgment of some nations and people who now exist. This should cause us both to mourn and rejoice. People opposed to God desperately need to hear the gospel. Judgment has been prophesied and is coming. This also means that the evil we see around us will not last forever. It will meet its end. Jesus will have victory.

QUESTIONS

List out all the things you know about Egypt—the things they did to God's people and the ways they forsook God Himself. How does Isaiah 19:16-24 teach you about the power of God's redemption?

How does chapter 20 illustrate that the only help that we have comes from the Lord?

Reread Isaiah 21:9b-10. Since Babylon represents the world, what kinds of idols does the world worship? Do you tend to give worship to any of these idols as well? To what does the passage teach us that idol worship leads?

Isaiah 22-24

After God proclaims His coming judgment for the people of Babylon, He turns toward His people, the northern kingdom of Israel.

What is heartbreaking about Isaiah 22 is that it shows that Israel has become almost identical to other nations of which God wanted them to be so different. This prophecy was given a century and a half before it came to fruition, which shows us that they had become hardened in their sin. The Lord desired for them to repent, mourn over their sin, and turn to Him, but instead, they feasted and indulged themselves in worldly pleasures. Israel was no different than Babylon. The chosen people of God had become like the world. The Lord says in His judgment that there would be no deliverance for them (Isaiah 22:14). This is a harsh reality for Israel, but unlike the other nations, they had access to God's truth and wisdom, and they chose to reject Him. Though the Lord graciously desires for all to be saved and has made a way for their salvation, people still reject Him today, and they will meet the same fate as the Israelites who rejected God.

The Lord then specifically condemns a wicked man named Shebna who had authority during the time of Isaiah, and He promises that a man named Eliakim will rise up and faithfully lead God's people (Isaiah 22:15-25). However, even Eliakim will fall short, which points the people of God to their need for a Savior who will hold "the key of the house of David" and give the people eternal security (Isaiah 22:22). This key will be held by Christ (Revelation 3:7). Only Christ can deliver us!

The Lord gives another judgment for the nation of Tyre in Isaiah 23. Tyre was proud because they were a very wealthy and powerful trading city in the Mediterranean. It would be seemingly impossible to defeat Tyre because of their defensive position on the sea. Tyre represents the lust for worldly possessions and greed for earthly power and wealth. Satan is even referred to as "the king of Tyre" in Ezekiel 28:11-19. Tyre and Babylon represent the world's desires and pride, and the prince of this world loves when mankind puts faith in such things apart of God. The Lord promises in Isaiah 23:18 that the wealth of Tyre will eventually be inherited by God's people. In Christ, the humble will inherit the earth, not those who are greedy and lust after wealth (Matthew 5:5). When we follow Jesus, our treasure is in His heavenly kingdom.

"When we follow Jesus, our treasure is in His heavenly kingdom."

Isaiah 24 contains an apocalyptic prophecy for the judgment of the entire world. Even though this prophecy gives followers of Christ hope, it also should stir us to action for the sake of the gospel. While we will someday sing songs of praise to Christ "from the ends of the earth," there will be many who will be separated from Christ forever (Isaiah 24:16). We will someday see the wrath of God defeat Satan forever, and God will bring His kingdom to earth. Man and God will finally dwell together again.

QUESTIONS

Reread Isaiah 22:22-25. How does knowing that all of this is spoken from the Lord help us understand the importance of the book of Isaiah?

What does Isaiah 23:17 illustrate about both God and man?

In chapter 24, we read that God's judgment will be implemented on the earth. How and why is God's judgment a good thing?

Isaiah 25-27

Isaiah 25 and 26 document a refreshing and hopeful song from the faithful remnant of God's people.

This song displays the Lord's goodness and provision through His redemptive plan for all mankind. In Isaiah 25, the people of Judah get a glimpse of the wonderful things He is going to do through Christ (Isaiah 25:1). The foreign nations who come against Israel will be humbled, but even then, God will allow some of these people to know Him (Isaiah 25:3). This reminds us of how the Lord has cared for everyone, not only the nation of Israel, all along. Even before God sent Christ to die for our sins, He provided a way for all people to know Him. The Lord will also not be like evil and oppressive leaders of the world who abuse the poor and needy. Instead, He will be their shelter, and the Lord will allow those who were once His enemies to find refuge in Him as well. The Lord will destroy "the burial shroud" that has been placed over every man and woman because of sin (Isaiah 25:7). The way the "burial shroud" is destroyed is through Jesus. Jesus will "swallow up death once and for all" through His perfect life, atoning death, and glorious resurrection (Isaiah 25:8).

The Lord has given Judah repeated promises of salvation, but in Isaiah 26, He will show them how to endure as they are waiting for these promises to come about. As the people lose their current home because of judgment, they must remember their true home is God's coming city (Isaiah 26:1). Isaiah says that if they keep their minds fixed on God, He will keep them in "perfect peace" (Isaiah 26:3). This peace is rooted in the knowledge that the Lord has accomplished salvation for them. In the same way, our peace comes from knowing that the Lord accomplished salvation for us through Christ (Isaiah 26:12, Ephesians 2:8-9). We are in exile in this world and do not belong here. As we are persecuted in the name of Jesus, we have hope in the resurrection of Christ and our future home in eternity (Isaiah 26:19).

Chapter 27 once again paints the picture of Israel as a vineyard. In the vineyard, God is watching over, watering, and destroying every sign of the curse (Isaiah 27:4). The vineyard is a metaphor for how the Lord watches over, nurtures, and protects Israel. In fact, this metaphor even makes it clear that He

"Our God redeems."

even offers peace to those who have once been in enmity with Him (Isaiah 27:5). Even in their weakness, He will provide a rescuer. Through this tiny nation, all nations will be blessed by Jesus—just as God promised to Abraham. Our God redeems. He uses even our weakness for His glory. He did it for Israel, and He can certainly do it for us as well.

QUESTIONS

What aspects of God's character do you see in chapters 25-26? List them below.

Meditate on Isaiah 26:12. What does this verse tell you about the relationships between our peace and the Lord's work?

Reread Isaiah 27:12-13. Then read Matthew 24:31 and Revelation 11:15. How do these cross-references help you understand the prophecy in this passage at the end of Isaiah 27?

Isaiah 28-30

In Isaiah 28, the Lord directs His attention from Judah to the northern kingdom of Israel.

They would face judgment for their rejection of the Lord, and their destruction was a warning to the people of Judah in the southern kingdom. The northern kingdom had become proud and drunk with the pleasure of the world (Isaiah 28:1). They forgot the Lord and the true treasure of being one of His children. Even the priests and prophets behaved wickedly and treated the Lord's words with contempt, so the Lord promised their coming judgment at the hands of the Assyrians (Isaiah 28:7, 11). However, through their judgment, Israel would recognize their sin and mistakes, and they would turn to the Lord (Isaiah 28:15). And He would give them salvation from death through the Messiah, who will bring righteousness and justice to all who believe in Him (Isaiah 28:16-18).

In Isaiah 29, the Lord details how Israel will be destroyed, but He promises that He would eventually avenge them and defeat their foreign enemy (Isaiah 29:5-7). This promise was fulfilled when the angel of the Lord killed 185,000 Assyrians (Isaiah 37:36-37). In the meantime, the people of Israel will "honor [God] with lip-service," yet they will be cold-hearted toward the Lord (Isaiah 29:13). Jesus points back to this verse when talking to the Pharisees in Matthew 15:7-8 when he says, "Hypocrites! Isaiah prophesied correctly about you when he said: This people honors me with their lips, but their heart is far from me." These words are just as relevant today as we sometimes desire to appear spiritually healthy, even when our hearts are not in the right place. However, when we struggle with feeling cold toward the Lord, we must remember who He is and what He has done. He has opened the eyes of the spiritually blind and made the deaf heart truth (Isaiah 29:18). And He has given the humble true joy in Him (Isaiah 29:19). When we are cold-hearted, we must repent and submit ourselves to the Lord. He will gladly renew within us a heart for serving Him (Psalm 51:10).

"The Lord loves to show graciousness and mercy to His people."

The northern kingdom of Israel was quick to place their faith in the things that they could see, but they struggled to trust the Lord. In Exodus, it was a golden calf, and here in Isaiah, it was the nation of Egypt (Exodus 32, Isaiah 30:1-2). Armies and military powers seemed secure to them. They did not recognize

that nations would rise and fall, but the Lord will reign forever. We, too, are quick to place our trust in earthly things such as political leaders, our families, those we look up to, or even in our own strength. However, the Lord promises that we will be saved when we return and rest in Him (Isaiah 30:15). The Lord loves to show graciousness and mercy to His people (Isaiah 30:18). God shows us through Isaiah that our preoccupation with the things of this world and even our self-sufficiency prevent us from seeing His provision.

QUESTIONS

Focus on Isaiah 28:16. Then read Matthew 21:33-46. How does understanding the context of Isaiah 28 help you understand why Jesus is quoting these words?

How does Matthew 15:8-9 expand your understanding of Isaiah 29:13?

What does Isaiah 30:18-22 teach you about the Lord's response to sinners who return to Him? How does this passage comfort you?

Isaiah 31-33

In chapter 31, the prophet again urges the people of Judah not to trust Egypt to save them from Assyria.

"We live in light of redemption and await the day when He will make everything right."

Judah saw Assyria conquer nation after nation, and they were afraid. It would be very tempting and easy to see visible signs of strength in horses and chariots and want to run toward them, but these visible signs were nothing compared to the power of the Lord. With a stretch of His hand, He could demolish any of Judah's enemies (Isaiah 31:3). They were all flesh, but the Lord is God. The Lord gives them a picture of how He will defend Israel by comparing Himself to a ferocious lion and a tender bird (Isaiah 31:4-5). Judah needs only to repent and return to the Lord, and He would act on their behalf. While we may look at Judah and wonder how they could put their trust in Egypt, the nation that once enslaved them, and not the Lord, we must remember that we do the same thing all the time. We look to wealth, people of affluence, our appearance, and even our careers for salvation. These are not bad things, but when we depend on them to deliver us, we misuse them and forget the hope we have in the Lord. We must be cautious about trusting in things of the world that are passing away instead of the Lord, who will remain forever.

At the beginning of chapter 32, Isaiah contrasts a righteous and foolish king. This prophecy was likely given during the reign of King Ahaz, who was one of the wicked kings of Judah. His son, Hezekiah, would eventually rule and fulfill this prophecy of a king reigning in righteousness. More than that, this prophesy ultimately points to Jesus, the true King of righteousness. Isaiah placed great emphasis on the peace that accompanies righteousness. There is no peace apart from Jesus and no righteousness in ourselves (Romans 3:10-20). He is our righteousness, and He is our peace.

Chapter 33 begins with a promise of Assyria's destruction. Judah had finally turned to the Lord for deliverance, but it had taken quite a blow. When King Hezekiah ruled over Judah, Sennacherib, the king of Assyria, took all of Judah's fortified cities. Hezekiah tried to buy off Sennacherib in order to save Judah from seemingly inevitable annihilation, but Sennacherib broke his word after receiving the money he demanded (2 Kings 18-19). Judah had nowhere else to turn but to the Lord, and even though they came to Him as a last resort, He still chose to deliver them (2 Kings 19:5-7). Finally, the Lord gives them the

gospel in the final verses of Isaiah 33. He reminds them that they are sinners and that none of them can dwell with Him, except He who is righteous (Isaiah 33:14-15). This righteous one is Christ, and He gives His people His righteousness so that they can dwell with God and be in His presence (Isaiah 33:16-17). If you believe in Christ, you are also a saved sinner who will one day behold Christ, the righteous King, in the eternal city of God. We live in light of redemption and await the day when He will make everything right.

QUESTIONS

Meditate on Isaiah 31:1, and spend some time in self-examination. Do you trust in and depend on the things of the world, or do you put your trust in the Lord?

What does chapter 32 teach you about the Lord's justice and discipline?

Spend some time in prayer in light of Isaiah 33:2. Ask that God would renew your strength in Him every day and deliver you from distress, replacing it with praise for Him and His faithfulness.

Isaiah 34-36

Our merciful God is also a God of justice. Isaiah 34 shows us the fate of those who reject God.

While the prophecy finds its first fulfillment in nations who come against Israel, it ultimately points to the judgment of everyone who turns their back on the Lord. "Edom" refers to the descendants of Esau, who was the older brother of Jacob. Edom is often used to describe those who will never believe in Jesus for salvation and thus are not part of the elect of God (Isaiah 34:5, 6, 9, Romans 9). This passage should stir our hearts with compassion toward our unbelieving friends and family members. There is much more at stake than our fear of rejection when we share the gospel. Judgment is coming. It has been ordained by God and is already written (Isaiah 34:16-17).

However, the judgment of the world will also be accompanied by the jubilant song of the redeemed. There is hope amidst sorrow. The song reminds us of the nation of Israel when they first entered the promised land. And this song also looks ahead to the future and the certainty that Jesus will come again and make all things new. God will restore the universe, and the curse on the ground will be no more (Isaiah 35:1-2). The earth and all creation will cease groaning from the burden of sin and will instead rejoice (Romans 8:18-25). The earth will be filled with the glory of the Lord (Isaiah 35:2). After explaining how the earth will be filled with glory, Isaiah transitions to talking about Israel's restoration. That said, Isaiah 35:4 can be understood in multiple ways. First, the Lord will bring the ransomed of Judah back from captivity to their home. Second, the Lord will send His Son, Jesus, to die for the sins of His people so they can be saved. Finally, the Lord has an established day when Jesus will return and defeat sin and death forever, and all the people of God will finally be home. Someday, Isaiah 34:8-10 will be our reality. We will sing with the redeemed people of Israel as we enter the eternal city of God. We will live there forever, and our joy in Christ will never end.

"There is hope amidst sorrow."

Isaiah 36 shifts from prophecy to a historical narrative to recount the enmity between Assyria and Judah. King Sennacherib of Assyria had sent his field commander, Rabshakeh, and a great army to the last standing city of Judah, which was Jerusalem. Rabshakeh comes against Hezekiah and the Lord with wicked and evil words and calls all of the people of Judah to rely on Assyria in-

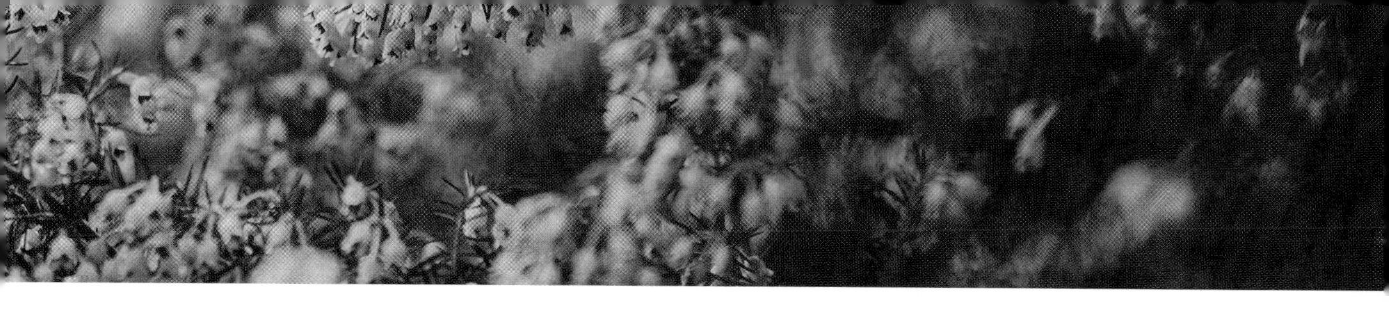

stead of their God and king. The attacks of Rabshakeh are no different than Satan's attacks today, and even though it may seem in certain situations that all is lost, we must believe that the Lord is our Deliverer. There is no power greater than Him, no matter how threatening someone may appear. When Satan attacks us with words of deception, we should be like the officials from Hezekiah's government who refused to answer Rabshakeh and refuse to answer Satan. Instead, we should look to Christ for help, knowing He is greater than Satan, who is the prince of this world.

QUESTIONS

After reading through chapter 34, what are some ways that God's judgment and discipline are good for His people? List them below.

Reflect on Isaiah 35. How does this song give you hope? How does it cause you to look forward?

Reread Isaiah 36:18-20. Why is the God of Israel far more trustworthy than the gods of the surrounding nations? Why can we always trust that the Lord will come through for us?

Isaiah 37-39

In these chapters, Isaiah continues to give pieces of the historical backdrop of the prophecies.

When Hezekiah hears the King of Assyria's message, he tears his clothes and puts on a sackcloth. He goes to the house of the Lord and tells his officials to ask Isaiah to plead to God for deliverance. When the men come to Isaiah, he immediately tells them that God is going to destroy Sennacherib. But Sennacherib sends one final message to Hezekiah, telling him not to believe the Lord because He is lying about saving Jerusalem. Sennacherib has been able to defeat all other gods of the nations he has conquered—why is the God of Israel any different? This is utter blasphemy. Sennacherib is accusing God of something that characterizes Satan: deceit. And he is doing the same thing Satan did to Adam and Eve by asking Hezekiah and the people of Judah to question the Word of God.

The king of Assyria mistakenly compares the living God to man-made, worthless idols of wood and clay (Isaiah 37:19). God will not be mocked, and Sennacherib heaped destruction onto himself by his words (Galatians 6:7-8). Hezekiah prays fervently to the Lord, and the Lord answers. 185,000 Assyrians fall at the hand of the angel of the Lord. The angel of the Lord is often thought to be Christ before He became flesh in the New Testament. If this is so, what an incredible foreshadowing of what Jesus accomplished on the cross and what He will do when He someday returns to earth. On the cross, Jesus destroyed the power of sin and death, and when He returns, He will annihilate sin and death forever.

"Jesus is the only one who rules in perfect righteousness."

King Hezekiah was a good king for most of his reign and brought the nation back to the Lord. However, serving the Lord is not a guarantee that we will never have trouble. God uses the Assyrian invasion to remind His people and Hezekiah to trust in Him alone. And when Hezekiah becomes ill in Isaiah 38, He will have to lean on the Lord and trust Him again. Hezekiah begs the Lord to spare his life. The Lord hears Hezekiah's pleas and adds fifteen years to Hezekiah's life.

Despite all of this, one of the last recorded events of Hezekiah's reign shows him allying with Babylon, the very nation that would one day carry Judah

into captivity, instead of putting His trust in the Lord (Isaiah 39). And when Isaiah rebuked Hezekiah for this and told him of the coming judgment of Judah and his household, his only response was that he was glad it would not happen during his lifetime. Hezekiah had become prideful and self-centered. While he was one of Judah's righteous kings, he was not the perfect righteous King. Jesus is the only one who rules in perfect righteousness, and He will provide true and lasting deliverance for His people.

QUESTIONS

Reread Hezekiah's prayer in Isaiah 37:16-20. What do we learn from this prayer?

What does God's response to Hezekiah in Isaiah 37:22-29 tell us about who He is?

Paraphrase King Hezekiah's poem in 38:10-20.

Isaiah 40-42

We have read Isaiah's prophetic judgments and historical backdrops for the last 39 chapters of this book.

Finally, in Isaiah 40 and 41, we are given passages that are devoted to God's forgiveness, power, and tender care for His people. It is a fresh glimpse of who our God is. He is the One who comforts His people (Isaiah 40:1). He is the one in control of the whole world (Isaiah 40:22-26, Isaiah 41:2). He is the Good Shepherd who calls us by name (Isaiah 40:11, Isaiah 41:8). He gives strength to the weary (Isaiah 40:28-31). And amazingly, in Isaiah 40:2, we find that He will offer forgiveness for the sins of His people. This truth also points to the fact that our glorious and majestic God has chosen to bestow kindness to weak, incapable sinners through salvation in Jesus Christ. He does not just forgive us; He puts His love on us. These chapters remind us that because God is loving and just, we do not need to worry or fear. He will not leave us alone. He will walk with us every step of the way and will give us everything we need to face this life.

Isaiah 40 and 41 also encourage us to remember that the earth and all in it are passing away, but the Lord and His Word stand forever (Isaiah 40:6-8, Isaiah 41:2, 11-12). It is strange to think that after we die, hardly anyone will remember who we were and what we did. And even though we will no longer be on the earth, the Lord's Word will be, and it will go forth to aid believers just like it is now! Our mortality shows us our limitations and pushes us to rely on our Heavenly Father, who is unchanging and unlimited.

Chapter 42 contains an introduction of "the servant of the Lord." This servant will be a righteous, gentle King, unlike the evil and wicked kings of the earth. Though the original readers would not understand who this king is, we know that this gentle servant king is Jesus. Verse 3 points us to Jesus's immense mercy—He will not break the bruised reed or quench the faintly burning wick. Jesus is a refuge for the weary and a shelter for those bruised by the world. He has not come to wound the wounded or break the broken but to heal and comfort (Mark 2:17). He piles the kindling around our faint hearts and kindles the flame with His love. There is healing, mercy, grace, and life to be found in the name of Jesus.

"There is healing, mercy, grace, and life to be found in the name of Jesus."

QUESTIONS

Meditate on Isaiah 40:1. What do you think the significance is of this opening statement?

How do these chapters help you to better understand the power of God?

Spend some time in self-examination in light of Isaiah 42:18-25. In what ways can we be like Israel?

Isaiah 43-45

The nation of Israel rebelled and rejected the Lord. And yet, in Isaiah 43, the Lord speaks words of love and promise over His people.

The first few verses of this passage contain precious promises for Judah and followers of Christ. The Lord promises that He will be with us whenever we pass through overwhelming waters and fires. Water and fire often symbolized God's judgment in the Old Testament, but they become signs of new life in the New Testament (John 4:10-26, Acts 2). The Lord also promises Judah that He will work on their behalf and deliver them. Just as He had made a way for Israel's deliverance in the past, He promises in Isaiah 43:19-21 to make a way for His chosen people again. While the Lord does sustain Israel during their exile and eventually restores them to their home, this "new thing" points to God's plan of salvation in the new covenant of Christ. God would atone for the sins of His people forever through Christ's death on the cross (Isaiah 43:25).

"The Lord is our powerful Redeemer, and He is God alone."

At the beginning of Isaiah 44, God promises to pour out His Spirit among His people. We have seen this promise before in Isaiah, and it shows how God will take people who are broken and hardened in sin and give them new hearts (Ezekiel 11:19). The outpouring of God's Spirit will cause His chosen people to "spring up" all around the world (Isaiah 44:4). They will call themselves by the Lord's name and identify as His children (Isaiah 44:5). This is the hope we have received in the gospel. We have received the Spirit of God and are called a son or daughter of God. When we know Him, we will see the foolishness of looking to anyone or anything else to give us salvation. The Lord is our powerful Redeemer, and He is God alone (Isaiah 44:6-7).

And while the Lord is the Redeemer of His people, He allows human leaders to be part of His mission of salvation for the people of Judah. God declares that Cyrus, the King of Persia, would deliver His people from the hands of Babylon, even though Cyrus was a pagan and did not know the Lord (Isaiah 45:1-6). The Lord makes this promise nearly a century before Cyrus rises to power. Cyrus would be an instrument in the Lord's hand, and the Lord would enable him to have victory over the nations. While God's people were still rebelling, He was making a way of deliverance from their future judgment. However, Cyrus would only be a shadow of the true and great deliverer, Jesus.

QUESTIONS

What do you think it means when God says that He will be with Israel when they pass through the waters and through the fire in Isaiah 43:2?

Spend some time reflecting on Isaiah 44:6-23. Are you prone to worship idols? What are some things that you tend to love and serve more than the Lord?

How does Isaiah 45:9 expand your understanding of trusting in the Lord's plan?

Isaiah 46-48

Though the Lord had loved and cherished the people of Israel, their hearts were stubborn and quick to go their own way.

They fashioned idols and carried them around, looking to them for help that only the Lord could provide (Isaiah 46:1-2). The idols the people made were doomed to the same judgment and fate that the people of Judah faced. They would be carried into a foreign land, and the idols would be unable to save the people from disaster. Judah carried their idols, but the Lord carried them (Isaiah 46:3-4). The Lord had been with His people since their birth, and He would be with them until they were old and grey. It is the same for us today. The idols of this world will never satisfy us or carry us through the pain and suffering of this life. Only God can do that! We are unable to achieve righteousness or salvation for ourselves, and so God acts on our behalf through the person of Jesus. He covers us with the righteousness of His beloved Son and makes us His own (Isaiah 46:12-13). We must lay down the idols of our hearts that we vainly place our trust in and run to the One who is worthy of our worship. It is at His feet that we will find the peace and satisfaction the world could never give.

In Isaiah 47, God tells Babylon that they will fall under His hand into judgment. While the Lord used Babylon to accomplish His will for the people of Judah, Babylon was prideful and put themselves in place of God (Isaiah 47:8). The Lord will also show these people that He alone is God. Babylon is the city that symbolizes the world or people who reject God, and their actions and thoughts in this chapter imitate the "prince of this world," Satan. However, the people who reject God and Satan will meet the same end as the original city of Babylon: they will be burned in a consuming fire (Isaiah 47:14, Revelation 20:10). God acts on behalf of His people and brings their enemies to ruin, and God will one day completely wipe away evil from the earth when Christ returns.

"He is patient and merciful."

The Lord tells His people in Isaiah 48 that He has told them how He will save them so that they will not claim His glorious works as a result of idol worship. He wants them to know that He is the only one who can accomplish salvation

for them (Isaiah 48:3-5). The Lord desires their hearts, and though they rebel against Him again and again, He is patient and merciful (Isaiah 48:9-10). Even though they wander, He saves them and gives them the peace and righteousness they could never have on their own (Isaiah 48:18). This is a picture of the gospel of Jesus, where God is glorified by saving sinners and giving them salvation.

QUESTIONS

Meditate on Isaiah 46:3-4. How can this bring you encouragement today?

How can the warnings to the pagan nations in chapter 47 also serve as reminders to us to remain holy?

Focus on Isaiah 48:17-19. Why do you think leadership of and instruction from the Lord are good for us?

Isaiah 49-51

As the songs about the coming Servant of God continue, we see more promises of Christ's coming and can rejoice in how He fulfills them.

Isaiah 49 shows us an incredible picture of a conversation between the Lord and the Servant Messiah, who is Jesus. The Lord tells the Servant about His mission and what He will accomplish on earth. This picture of Jesus takes our breath away as we see how He has fulfilled every one of these promises (Luke 24:44). Though the people of Israel had failed in their role as God's servant, this Servant would be perfect. He would be a light to the nations and would extend salvation to the ends of the earth (Genesis 12:3, Isaiah 2:1-4, Matthew 28:16-20). Jesus would be the restorer of the redeemed people of God. Not only would God bring restoration for the people to their homeland, but through Jesus, we can all experience ultimate restoration to God.

In Isaiah 50, Christ responds to the conversation between Him and the Lord in the previous chapter. He will perfectly obey what His Father has asked Him to do, despite suffering at the hand of the people He came to save (Isaiah 50:4-6). Jesus knows His Father is with Him and will seek His Father's help (Isaiah 50:7). The Lord desires obedience from His people. Israel and Judah rebelled against Him, but He still sought to save and restore them to Himself. Jesus will be the greater Israel who will do everything His Father asks of Him. He will even die on the cross for the sake of God's remnant people, and He will extend salvation to the world. Because of Christ's obedience, we can obey our Heavenly Father. The Servant Messiah, Jesus, has allowed us to become servants of the Most High God.

God's salvation of Judah points to the salvation that will come for all of God's people through Jesus Christ. The Lord will fulfill His promise to restore Judah to their homeland. And, someday, He will bring all people who love Jesus to the eternal city of Zion (Isaiah 51:3). The earth and all that is in it is passing away, but the salvation of God will stand forever (Isaiah 51:6). As we observe and remember all of the ways He has been faithful, we can joyfully look toward the day when He will bring us to our eternal home—God's redemptive plan will be complete (Isaiah 51:11). This is the hope that keeps us from trusting in the world and looking to its pleasures to fulfill us. Everlasting joy is coming!

"Everlasting joy is coming!"

QUESTIONS

What do these chapters tell you about Jesus Christ?
What significance do these things have?

How does Isaiah 50:9-10 teach you to grow in your confidence in the Lord?

How does Isaiah 51:11 reflect the joy that we will have when we are ushered home into the new heavens and new earth?

Isaiah 52-54

While Isaiah 52 primarily refers to the return and salvation of the people of Judah from Babylon, its fuller meaning is found in the final redemption of God's people as they enter the eternal city of Zion.

"We are clothed in the righteousness of Jesus."

The wicked and unclean, those who have rejected God, will not be able to enter (Isaiah 52:1). The family of God will be at peace. God tells the people of Judah that they will be "redeemed without silver," but this does not mean their redemption has no cost (Isaiah 52:3). God's people will all ultimately be redeemed by the blood of Jesus Christ (1 Peter 1:18-19). This is the gospel! Isaiah prophesies that this good news of the gospel will go out into the world and mountains by the beautiful feet of those who believe (Isaiah 52:7). In the New Testament, Jesus is the first one who brings this good news to us, but all who love Him follow after His example. We join His ministry peace as we bring good news and proclaim salvation to the world.

Isaiah 53 is the climax of the book of Isaiah, and the foreshadowed cross of Christ is the climax of all of history. The words of Isaiah 53 are quoted in the New Testament more than any other passage from the Old Testament. This stunning picture of the Messiah points so clearly to Jesus, who would fulfill every word of this prophecy, a prophecy that was written seven centuries before He was born! Here, we see a picture of our Savior, and we are left in awe of all that He has done for us. He did not suffer because He was guilty but because we were guilty (Isaiah 53:4-6). He is our substitution. He is the one who took what we deserved so that we could go free, and the result of His suffering is our peace and healing. Jesus changes everything. The sacrifice of Jesus brings peace to God's people and is an invitation of salvation to the nations. He has loved us with an everlasting love, and He has accomplished what we could have never done on our own. Jesus, the Suffering Servant, is our Messiah.

After revealing what the Messiah will one day do for the people of God, the Lord calls His people to rejoice. For they were once like a barren woman who was ashamed and rejected by her husband, but now she has been restored and brought back (Isaiah 54:1, 4-8). The Lord is this faithful husband to His people, and He delights in putting His mercy and compassion on them and showing

them everlasting love. The Lord gives His people a picture of what they can look forward to since they belong to Him (Isaiah 54:9-17). Their righteousness will forever be established, and they will experience a covenant of peace with the Lord. This is what has been given to followers of Christ. We are clothed in the righteousness of Jesus, and we have eternal peace with God because of Christ's suffering on the cross. We belong to the Lord.

QUESTIONS

Focus on Isaiah 52:7. What is this verse talking about?
How can we apply this idea in our lives now?

In what ways does Jesus fulfill the prophecies in chapter 53? List them below.
Hint: If you are new to reading the Bible, check out Matthew 8:17 and John 12:38.

Paraphrase Isaiah 54:17 in your own words.

Isaiah 55-57

Isaiah 55 opens with a tender call from the Lord for His people to return to Him. And this call is not just for Judah but for "everyone who is thirsty" for the Lord (Isaiah 55:1).

"He opens our eyes to see our wickedness and to accept the gospel of peace."

The Lord asks the people why they spend their money on things that will never satisfy them when He offers Himself and His everlasting covenant free of charge (Isaiah 55:2-3). The Lord will not only satisfy them, but He will pardon all of the sins of those who desire Him. He will have compassion on those who once rejected Him! This is astounding and almost unbelievable, especially in light of His coming judgment. Yet, God's redemptive purposes in Christ are better than anything we could ever imagine! Because of what Jesus has done, the call is simple: come. All who are weary, all who are poor, and all who are thirsty are invited to come to Jesus, who can satisfy all of our needs (John 4:10-14).

The Lord's heart for the nations is on full display in Isaiah 56 as God again promises that His salvation and righteousness are coming and will be extended to all people (Isaiah 56:1, 7). The Lord's promise for the Gentiles that follow Him—even those who live in ways contrary to laws given in the book of Leviticus, known as the Levitical law—is that they will be given an everlasting name that is better than the title of "sons and daughters" (Isaiah 56:5). They shall dwell in the house of God (Isaiah 56:7). This would have been absolutely incredible for the people to hear because this would mean that the very people who delivered Judah into exile would have an opportunity to follow God. This text points to the new covenant that God promises in the Old Testament and fulfills in Christ. The new covenant is where God promises to forgive our sins and restore us to Himself through the death and resurrection of Jesus.

In Isaiah 57, the Lord compares the lives of the righteous to the lives of the wicked. Though calamity could take away a righteous man, death is not something that worries them because the death of a righteous person sends them to the presence of God (Isaiah 57:2). Belonging to the Lord and walking in righteousness gives a person eternal peace and rest. However, the wicked who pursue the idols of the world have no lasting security because their

idols can do nothing on their behalf (Isaiah 57:13). In contrast, the Kings of kings, our Holy God, offers us Himself as a refuge (Isaiah 57:13, 15). He opens our eyes to see our wickedness and to accept the gospel of peace, but those who remain hardened in their wickedness will know no such peace, even though the Lord desires for them to have the gospel and be saved (Isaiah 57:18-21, 2 Peter 3:9).

QUESTIONS

Read John 4:10-14. How does this passage relate to Isaiah 55?

In what ways does Isaiah 55 offer us encouragement to pursue God in whatever state we are in?

What does Isaiah 57:14-21 tell us about the nature of God and the ways in which we should behave toward Him?

Isaiah 58-60

Throughout Israel's history, there were times when the people followed the Lord and times when they did what was right in their own eyes.

Isaiah 58 refers to the people doing what was technically right, but their hearts were far from the Lord as they did so. God wanted His people to live and serve Him with pure hearts, but the people instead simply went through the religious motions of what they thought they should do. They did not imitate the Lord in caring for the needy and oppressed and instead lived for themselves (Isaiah 58:3-5). When we care for others' needs and live out Christ's call to "love one another," we are fulfilling our role as His ambassadors to a watching world (John 13:34-35). And when we choose to pour out our lives for others, we find satisfaction in God alone, and this leads us to rest and delight in Him (Isaiah 58:10-14).

Isaiah 59 gives us a picture of the hopeless condition of mankind without God. Paul will later remind us of the sin of man and its devastating effects in Romans 3, and he will use Isaiah 59 to support what he says. Isaiah 59 tells us that our iniquities have caused a separation between the Lord and us, and we walk in gloom and are like "the dead" (Isaiah 59:2, 9-10). We do not know the truth (Isaiah 59:15). Since there was no man who was righteous, God intervened. In this hopeless chapter, the gospel is plainly foreshadowed as Isaiah prophesies that God's "own arm brought salvation" (Isaiah 59:16). The person described in verse 17 is clearly Christ, as He is the only one who lives righteously and gives His people salvation. Jesus is the Redeemer who destroyed the power of sin, which absolved the iniquity that separated us from the Father.

"Jesus is the Redeemer who destroyed the power of sin."

And because Christ destroyed sin's power, we are set free from the curse of sin and can see the truth of the gospel. The Lord opens our eyes, softens our hearts, and gives us salvation through His Son. Earth is no longer our home. We belong to a future heavenly city. The glory of this city and all we have to look forward to is described in Isaiah 60. While this prophecy first can be applied to Judah's return from exile, the text points us, and the people who first heard it, to a glorious deliverance. The gospel will draw people from every nation, even those who are most hostile to the Lord (Isaiah 60:7). There will no longer be violence and suffering. The city of God will be full of peace and righteousness, and the Lord will be our light (Isaiah 60:17-22, Revelation 22:5).

QUESTIONS

Meditate on Isaiah 58:11. What does this teach you about the Lord's faithfulness? How does this show you our need for God?

Reread Isaiah 59:21, and spend some time reflecting on the faithfulness of God's covenant. How can this bring you comfort and encouragement today?

Read John 8:12 and then Isaiah 60:20. How does the verse in John help you to understand the verse in Isaiah?

Isaiah 61-63

Despite Israel's sin and rejection of the Lord, God promised deliverance through a Messiah.

"Our Savior will one day put to end the evil that has left our world cursed and broken."

Isaiah 61 announces the good news of the work of the Messiah. He will "bring good news to the poor," "heal the brokenhearted," "proclaim liberty to the captives and freedom to the prisoners," and "proclaim the year of the Lord's favor" (Isaiah 61:1-2). The language of Isaiah 61 would have been familiar to the Jews in the context of the year of Jubilee, which was a year of rest that occurred at the end of a seven-year cycle. During the year of Jubilee, prisoners were set free, and debts were forgiven. Jesus is the fulfillment of the year of Jubilee, and He will say this Himself when He goes to teach in the synagogue of His hometown (Luke 4:16-30). In Christ, we are set free, and our debts are forgiven. We are also given true rest in Christ, and our salvation in Christ points us to the rest we will have forever in eternity. The good news and work of the Messiah change our status from a sinner separated from God to a priest who belongs to God (Isaiah 61:6). In the Old Testament, only priests stood between the presence of God in the temple and the ordinary Israelites. So the fact that we are called "priests" means that Jesus gives us access to God. The Lord takes away our shame, and instead, He clothes us with "a robe of righteousness" (Isaiah 61:10). This is the righteousness that we can only have because of Christ. Though we have sinned against Him, He changes our hearts and calls us His own.

In Isaiah 62, the Lord promises His faithful remnant that because He has saved them, He will set them apart in righteousness. God will call His future heavenly kingdom by a new name. And, the inhabitants of this kingdom will be like "a glorious crown in the Lord's hand" (Isaiah 62:3). Because Christ has saved us, He delights in us like "a groom rejoices over his bride" (Isaiah 62:5). Our salvation in Christ means that we are part of the bride of Christ, which is His church, and we will one day be reunited with our heavenly bridegroom. Until the Lord establishes this heavenly kingdom, members of the bride of Christ must be like the watchmen of Jerusalem who intercede in prayer for the church as we eagerly await our future home in this broken world (Isaiah 62:6-7). And the church must also follow the command of Christ to go into all the world and spread the good news of the gospel. By doing this, we will follow Isaiah's prophecy that speaks of God's people clearing stones and building a highway into God's heavenly kingdom. This highway is an invitation to all the world's people to accept God's salvation (Isaiah 62:10-12), for the day of the Lord's

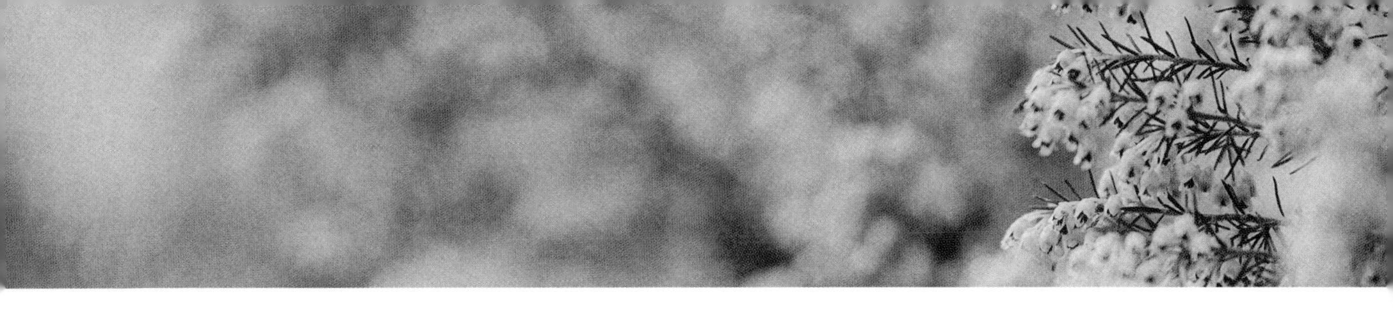

vengeance is coming. Isaiah 61:2 says that the Messiah will proclaim "the day of our God's vengeance." Isaiah 61:2 is one of the few prophecies in Isaiah that was not fulfilled in Jesus's first coming but will instead find fulfillment in His second coming. One day, Jesus will return to earth and bring terrible vengeance on the enemies of God (Revelation 19). He is the one Isaiah describes as wearing a robe stained with blood from the battle against sin, evil, and death (Isaiah 63:3-6). This description of Christ is repeated in Revelation 19 when John, the author of Revelation, writes, "He wore a robe dipped in blood, and his name is called the Word of God" (Revelation 19:13). These verses should cause us to tremble for those who reject Jesus. It should also stir us to share the good news of Christ with those who do not believe, as well as cause us to feel relieved. Our Savior will one day put to end the evil that has left our world cursed and broken.

QUESTIONS

Meditate on Isaiah 61:8. Why is it important to know what the Lord loves and hates?

What does Isaiah 62:4 teach you about the power of the Lord's healing and redemption?

Spend some time in self-examination and prayer in light of Isaiah 63:15-19. How do the words of Israel's prayer of repentance and lament speak truth into your own prayer life?

Isaiah 64-66

Beginning in the middle of Isaiah 63 to the end of Isaiah 64, a new narrator speaks.

This passage contains a prayer from one of Judah's exiles who is interceding for Israel. The term "interceding" means that he was praying to God on behalf of the people. In Isaiah 63, he remembers God's lovingkindness, mercy, and faithful works. He pleads for the Lord to show mercy to his people. And in Isaiah 64, this intercessor calls for God to work mightily again as He has before. He admits that the people have sinned against the Lord, and He asks the Lord not to remember their iniquity forever. Their home, the land where the people of Judah and their ancestors praised the Lord, was in ruins. The intercessor asks God to act on their behalf and not be silent toward this destruction. The intercessor's prayer will ultimately be answered in Christ, who will accomplish salvation for God's people and display the mightiness of God through His life, death, and resurrection. He will allow the iniquity of the redeemed to be forgiven.

In Isaiah 65, the Lord responds to this prayer. He has always wanted to be sought out and found by His people, which shows us His amazing grace, but His people rebelled against Him and walked in their own wickedness. They provoked the Lord and committed gross offenses that displayed their rejection of God. And because God is holy, there had to be consequences for these sins. But not all of Judah partook in this rejection of God. There is a faithful remnant of people who will not be destroyed in exile, and the Lord will bring them home. They would experience rich blessings from God, but those who rejected Him would be destined for eternal destruction. The Lord gives this faithful remnant of Israel a glimpse of the new world that is coming when the presence of sin is finally destroyed. Isaiah 65:17-22 shows us a picture of the millennial kingdom, which is the kingdom of Christ reigning on the earth. While many believers disagree about when this kingdom will take place, the words of this passage cause us to trust that our future in Christ is full of beauty, hope, and restoration. God will be with His people, and we will be at peace, forever.

"Our God saves!"

As the book of Isaiah ends, the Lord reminds His people that His desire is for them to understand who He is and come to Him in humility and brokenness

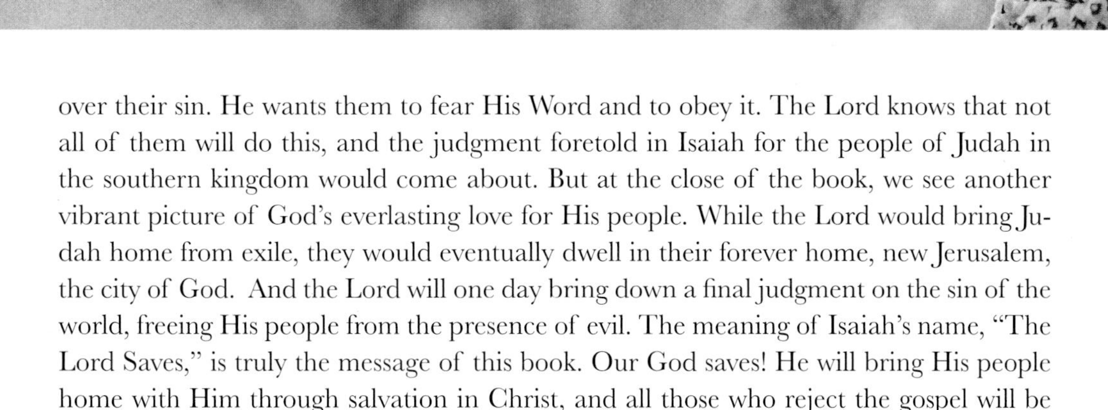

over their sin. He wants them to fear His Word and to obey it. The Lord knows that not all of them will do this, and the judgment foretold in Isaiah for the people of Judah in the southern kingdom would come about. But at the close of the book, we see another vibrant picture of God's everlasting love for His people. While the Lord would bring Judah home from exile, they would eventually dwell in their forever home, new Jerusalem, the city of God. And the Lord will one day bring down a final judgment on the sin of the world, freeing His people from the presence of evil. The meaning of Isaiah's name, "The Lord Saves," is truly the message of this book. Our God saves! He will bring His people home with Him through salvation in Christ, and all those who reject the gospel will be separated from Him forever.

QUESTIONS

Reread Isaiah 65:17-25. In what ways does this show you the hope that we have as believers in and coheirs with Christ?

Paraphrase Isaiah 66:12-17 in your own words.

Now that you have finished reading Isaiah, what are some of the things you have learned about God? What are some of the major themes present in this book?

This is
the Lord's
declaration.

Jeremiah

GENRE: *Prophet, Pre-exilic*

AUTHOR / DATE WRITTEN

Jeremiah • c. 640-580 BC

Warning Israel of Impending Judgment, Hope and Grace Following Discipline

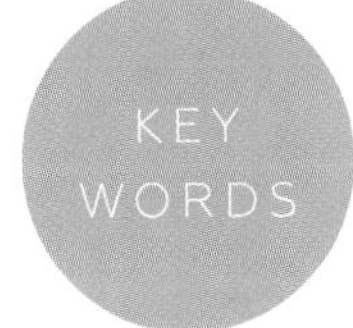

Judgment, Repentance, Covenant, Exile

KEY VERSE

JEREMIAH 31:31

'Look, the days are coming'—this is the Lord's declaration—'when I will make a new covenant with the house of Israel and with the house of Judah.'

Jeremiah 1-3

In the first chapter of the book of Jeremiah, we see the Lord call Jeremiah to speak His Words to the people of Israel.

Jeremiah is known as the weeping prophet, but we should remember him as a persevering prophet. In all of the years that he warned Israel of God's coming judgment, there were only two recorded converts. When he first began his ministry, he was a young man given a large and overwhelming task, but the Lord promised to lead him every step of the way. Jeremiah's life would not be easy. He would see Judah's destruction and judgment at the hand of the Babylonians that Isaiah prophesied nearly a hundred years earlier. Then, his countrymen would kidnap him and bring him to the land of Egypt. He would die there and never return home.

When we read Jeremiah's call with this knowledge of his life, the Lord's tender reminder not to be afraid because He would be near Jeremiah and deliver Him is even more meaningful. We are given these same promises as adopted sons and daughters of God. We are not guaranteed a carefree time on earth, but we are guaranteed His constant presence, even in the most difficult trials. Jesus has known us from the very beginning. He knew us before we were even born, and He has told us He will be us to the very end (Matthew 28:20). While we wait for the day when we will meet God face to face, He has prepared work for us to do just like He prepared work for Jeremiah so many years ago (Jeremiah 1:5, Ephesians 2:10).

The Lord does not waste time in giving Jeremiah a vision. The vision begins with Jeremiah seeing an almond branch. The almond tree was the first to bud in springtime. So when the Lord shows Jeremiah an almond branch and tells him that He will accomplish His Word, Jeremiah knows that He means that His judgment is coming soon (Jeremiah 1:11-12). Jeremiah's next vision of a boiling pot facing away from the north signifies that the judgment will come from the northern people of Babylon (Jeremiah 1:13-14). But in the same vision foreshadowing judgment, the Lord also promises Jeremiah's deliverance (Jeremiah 1:18). Jeremiah's life and persecution point us to Christ, who will weep on behalf of His people and be persecuted for what He says. Jesus's persecution, unlike Jeremiah's, will ultimately lead to our new life in Christ because it leads to His death and resurrection.

"He is our faithful Shepherd King."

In Jeremiah 2 and 3, the Lord reminds Judah of the covenant they have with Him as He describes Judah's faithlessness and idolatry. The people were living in rebellion and running to foreign gods and sinful practices, but the Lord urged them to return (Jeremiah 3:6-13). They had once delighted in the Lord like a new bride delights in her husband, but they had now forsaken Him (Jeremiah 2:2). They turned their back on "the fountain of living water" and created their own "cracked cisterns" (Jeremiah 2:13). When Jesus preaches the gospel, He calls Himself the fountain of living water, and He promises that anyone who follows Him would have rivers of living water as the overflow of their heart (John 4:13-14, John 7:38). He is our faithful Shepherd King who is promised at the end of Jeremiah 3 as the one who will bring full and final restoration to God's people (Jeremiah 3:15-18, John 10:11-14).

QUESTIONS

Focus on Jeremiah 1:6-10. What do these verses show you about the Lord?

Meditate on Jeremiah 2:13. How was what Israel had done evil? In what ways might we be prone to commit the same sins as Israel?

How does Jeremiah 3:11-13 remind you of what the Lord has done for you through the gospel?

Jeremiah 4-6

At the beginning of Jeremiah 4, the Lord shows the incredible result of Judah's repentance and return to Him—the nations would worship the Lord and come to know Him (Jeremiah 4:1-2).

God chose Israel to stand apart from all the nations so that the whole world would look to them and see how they lived and worshiped and be drawn to the Creator. However, they rebelled and rejected the Lord. Jesus would be the greater Israel who would draw all men and women chosen by God to Himself. When we follow Jesus, we enter into His kingdom of priests (which means that we have direct access to Him), but we can only properly worship the Lord because of Christ (1 Peter 2:9). Jeremiah anguished over the people's folly. He was known as the weeping prophet because his heart was broken and grieved over God's people's sin and brokenness. Jeremiah depicts God's judgment by using the same phrase Moses used in Genesis to describe the world before creation: "formless and empty" (Jeremiah 4:23). In a sense, the judgment on Judah will be a return to chaos and disorder like at the beginning of the world. The Lord will bring them through a new creation as they return to Him in the midst of their hardship and eventually go back to their homeland. Similarly, Jesus redeems us from the chaos and disorder of our sinful, earthly state and makes us new creations (2 Corinthians 5:17).

Chapter 5 and 6 of Jeremiah show us the devastating state of Judah and the city of Jerusalem. Though the Lord wants them to repent and return, there is no righteous person to be found (Jeremiah 5:1, 5). The Lord often compares Israel to a wild vine that does not bear proper fruit, and this should cause us to remember John 15 when Jesus calls Himself the true Vine (Jeremiah 5:10-11, John 15:5). Jesus will enable us to have the righteousness we could never possess on our own because He will live perfectly and obey His Father. And even though the people of Judah—from the young to the old, rejected the Lord—He would promise not to completely destroy them (Jeremiah 5:18). The Lord would preserve a faithful remnant of Israel. Even in His re-emphasis of judgment, He has mercy. This faithful remnant of Israel would contain the line from which the Messiah would eventually come, and this Messiah would deliver them from the fiercest enemies of all: sin and death.

"Jesus will enable us to have the righteousness we could never possess on our own."

QUESTIONS

What is the symbolism of "circumcising" the heart in Jeremiah 4:4? How does Romans 2:29 help you to understand this passage?

Reread Jeremiah 5:17-18. How does verse 18 display God's grace toward sinful people and His commitment to the covenant He made with Israel?

Paraphrase Jeremiah 6:10 in your own words.

Jeremiah 7-9

One of the repeated sentiments the Lord delivers to the people of Judah is that He has offered them the opportunity to repent again and again, but they would not.

"Only the gospel can save us from ourselves."

It is not that they are experiencing this judgment randomly. They have set it up for themselves by their evil deeds and idol worship, which they have also passed along to their children (Jeremiah 7:3, 18). This rebellion is not uncommon and has happened before, even after He delivered Israel from slavery in Egypt (Jeremiah 7:22-24). In Jeremiah's day, the people of Judah are just like the Israelites, dancing and feasting around the golden calf while Moses met with the Lord on top of the mountain (Exodus 32). They openly disobey God and choose their own gods and pleasure instead of Him. Even worse, the people of Judah are now sacrificing their children to false gods (Jeremiah 7:31). And just as God judged the people of Israel for their idol worship, He will judge the people of Judah. They will experience immense destruction and casualties at the hands of Babylon, and there will be piles of dead bodies after it is over. God does not spare the horrific details because the people of Judah have become so numb to their wickedness. However, when Jesus returns to judge the world, He will perfectly execute justice and destroy the wicked. Though much evil in our world appears to go unnoticed, it will be answered. Praise God that He has been merciful to us and saved us from ourselves. Let us urgently share this mercy with others because we know judgment is coming again.

In Jeremiah 8, the Lord says that the bones of the people killed by the Babylonians will lie before the objects of their worship, which are the sun, the moon, and all of the heavens (Jeremiah 8:1-2). This is the result of idol worship—death. The sun, moon, and stars will be able to do nothing for Judah as they are attacked, and the state of their desecrated bodies will be proof. The people had all fallen away, even the "wise men" who claimed to bring the people the word of God, but they only brought them messages filled with lies and deceit (Jeremiah 8:8-9). These wise men told the people what their ears wanted to hear. The idols the world turns to today also lead to spiritual death, and they cannot provide any salvation. Only the gospel can save us from ourselves. And while it is a beautiful message of peace and hope, it is also offensive or foolish to those

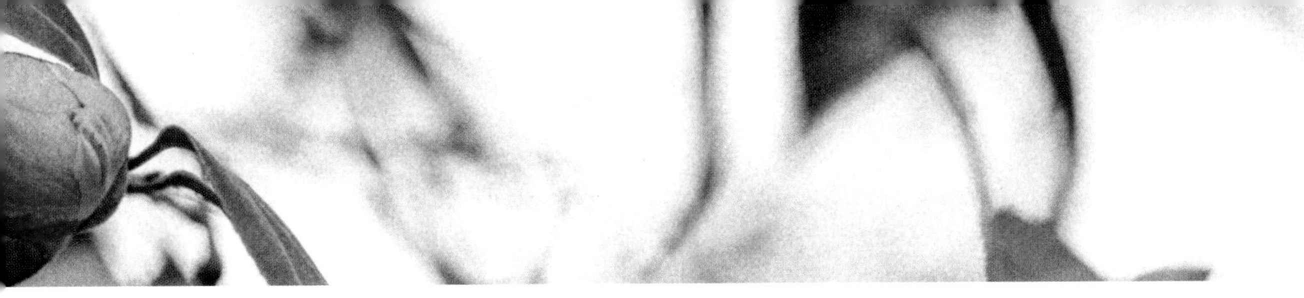

who do not believe (1 Corinthians 1:18). The gospel is not like the message of the wise man preaching to the wicked people of Judah. It calls out our sin and reveals our human condition, and because it does so, we can see our desperate need for Christ and His righteousness.

Jeremiah grieves deeply over the state of Judah because God will not spare them. Their fate is sealed. They have forsaken their covenant with the Lord and rejected Him, so now they will answer for their wrongdoing (Jeremiah 9:17-22). They were foolish and relied on themselves when true wisdom is only found in the Lord. We have been faithless as well. We are no better than the people of Judah, but Jesus has born God's wrath and allowed us to believe and know God.

QUESTIONS

Meditate on Jeremiah 7:8. Do we tend to do the same thing this verse describes? What are some practical action steps we can take to avoid this?

Reread Jeremiah 7:21-26. How does this passage convey to us the importance of obeying all that the Lord asks?

Look up the word "boast" in the dictionary, and then reread Jeremiah 9:23-24. How does this definition expand your understanding of this passage?

Jeremiah 10-12

The cure for Israel's idolatry is for them to glance at the beautiful character of God.

Jeremiah 10 is a stark reminder that there is none like Him. Who He is changes everything, and it most certainly changes us. The people had wandered far from God and had clung to idols while also pretending to still worship the Lord. They offered sacrifices in vain while their hearts were bowed to the idols of foreign lands. Our idols may look different, but the effect is the same. Though we may not worship statues of gold or wood, we are prone to worship our possessions, relationships, and a myriad of other things that try to claim first place in our hearts. And yet, our God is merciful and loving. He pursues us even when we have chosen the gift over the Giver and the creation over the Creator. He woos us back to Himself with unending grace and mercy, and He is ready and waiting to redeem every part of our story for our good and His glory.

In Jeremiah 11, the Lord tells Jeremiah to speak to the men of Judah and remind them that the promised curse is because they did not honor the covenant, which was their agreement with God. The language of their covenant would not be unfamiliar to them. They would have been told of what happened to their ancestors when they disobeyed God. But the men of Judah turned their backs on this truth, and idol worship filled the city that was supposed to be set apart for the Lord (Jeremiah 11:13). The Lord instructs Jeremiah not to pray for the people of Judah and to know that those who want to kill him for declaring the truth would be destroyed (Jeremiah 11:14, 21-23). While our God is gracious and merciful, He does not excuse sin. There will come a time when there will be no more opportunity for people to repent and turn to the Lord, and they will face destruction just like the people of Judah. This is a sober truth, but it is also comforting. Evil has a final day. While we ourselves were once wicked, our sin has been answered by the blood of Jesus. We will never be separated from the love of God (Romans 8:38-39).

"While we ourselves were once wicked, our sin has been answered by the blood of Jesus."

Jeremiah cries out to the Lord in chapter 12 over frustration that the wicked around him seems to be prospering. As a prophet who spoke the true Words of God, Jeremiah faced persecution and hardship. The Lord tells Jeremiah that

things will only worsen, but His judgment against Judah would be severe. However, there is a glimmer of hope at the end of this chapter as the Lord promises that He will again have compassion on Judah, and the nations who destroy them will answer for laying a hand on the Lord's people. But these nations would also have an opportunity to repent and come to know the Lord. God's judgment brings mercy. This is nowhere more evident than in the mercy that was extended to us through the death of Christ.

QUESTIONS

What are some things that you might be most prone to worship?
What are some active steps you can take to flee from that behavior?

Spend some time in prayer in light of Jeremiah 10:6, praising God that He is above all and thanking Him that there is no one as great, powerful, and good as He is.

Why do you think it was so important that the Israelites return to being faithful to their covenant with the Lord?

Jeremiah 13-15

In chapter 13, the Lord instructs Jeremiah to act out a parable for the people of Judah.

He tells Jeremiah to buy linen underwear, which was the noble cloth used by priests, and hide it in a rock by the Euphrates River (Jeremiah 13:4). When Jeremiah returned to retrieve the underwear at the Lord's command, it was ruined (Jeremiah 13:7). The Lord tells Jeremiah this is what He will do to Judah's pride. He will bring them low and disgrace them like the ruined underwear, and the only thing they will be able to do is the only thing the ruined underwear could still do—cling to something or someone. Judah will be forced to cling to the Lord (Jeremiah 13:11). He also has Jeremiah compare Judah to full bottles of wine. While full wine bottles can signify wealth and blessing, these full wine bottles symbolize the drunkenness of Judah. Instead of being blessed by the Lord, they will be like broken wine bottles dashed against each other (Jeremiah 13:13-14). The Lord then again clearly states the promise of their exile, and He mourns over how long it will be until His city of Jerusalem is made clean (Jeremiah 13:19, 27). We are like the ruined underwear and broken wine bottle apart from Christ. We are drunk with foolishness and ruined by our sin. We, like Judah, need to be cleansed. And, our only true salvation is found by clinging to Jesus.

Jeremiah 14 shows Judah dropping into disorder as they suffer from drought and famine. The Lord brings these conditions on the people to stir them to repentance. Jeremiah models what repentance should look like as He appeals to the Lord. He recognizes that the people of Judah have sinned, and he pleads for mercy. He states that the Lord is with them and asks for Him not to leave them, but the Lord again tells Jeremiah not to pray for the people. He will not accept their offerings or sacrifices, and they will face judgment.

The days of the prophet Jeremiah were incredibly difficult times, and Jeremiah 15 reveals the prophet's discouragement. The people hated Jeremiah—the people he so desperately wanted to help. Because of the wickedness of the people, they brought judgment on themselves. God did not enjoy the judgment of the people who He so deeply loved, but in His justice and holiness, He did what was right. And though Jeremiah did what the Lord had

"Our only true salvation is found by clinging to Jesus."

called him to do, the people would not listen. Jeremiah did not understand the situation in which he found himself, but the Lord called him to return, and He promised restoration. Jeremiah was faithful, even when it was hard. We are not immune to the discouragement and rejection that Jeremiah faced, but we can be assured of God's faithfulness. He will be faithful to redeem and restore all who return to Him. He was faithful to Jeremiah, and He will be faithful to us. He will never fail His redeemed people.

QUESTIONS

How is the Lord's warning in Jeremiah 13:15-20 something for us to reflect on today?

Reread Jeremiah 14:20-22. What does this passage teach you about repentance?

Summarize the conversation between Jeremiah and God in chapter 15.

Jeremiah 16-18

As the Lord describes the judgment coming upon the people of Judah, He compares it to silencing a wedding feast (Jeremiah 16:9).

Throughout Scripture, God describes Himself as a groom and His people as His bride. The silencing of joy at a wedding feast reveals great sadness and heartbreak. The Lord, the faithful groom, has been betrayed by Judah, His bride. What is even more saddening is that the people do not realize that they have betrayed the Lord. They are blind to their sin and do not understand the prophecies of judgment from Jeremiah (Jeremiah 16:10). They have become worse than their ancestors, who also rebelled against the Lord, and yet the Lord promises restoration (Jeremiah 16:12-15). He will deliver the people of Judah just like He delivered Israel from Egypt. This deliverance from the exile in Babylon will symbolize a second exodus, and it will foreshadow the coming exodus of all redeemed people from the bondage of sin because of the blood of Christ. The sin of Judah will be dealt with, so the hope of the Messiah and the fulfillment of God's covenant with Abraham, Moses, and David can be fulfilled.

Jeremiah uses the theme of the righteous man in Psalm 1 to illustrate the sin of Judah in chapter 17. The people placed their trust in men instead of in the Lord. However, kings, armies, and leaders could do nothing for them. The Lord longed for them to simply trust Him. The Lord says that the man who places his trust in other men is cursed, but the man who puts his faith in the Lord is blessed (Jeremiah 17:5, 7). We as humans are not naturally like the man described in Psalm 1, who places himself near the streams of the waters of the living God. We run from these waters and try to be self-sufficient. Whether we realize it or not, we attempt to supersede God when we do not depend on Him. We commit the same sin that Adam and Eve did in the garden when they desired to have the same knowledge and status as the Lord when all the while the Lord calls us to trust and rest. The righteous man in Psalm 1 and the sin of Judah illustrated in chapter 17 point us toward Jesus, the only person who was perfectly righteous. Our entire lives after we accept Christ as our Savior are spent in union and dependency on Him. We can do nothing without Him, and we become like the people of Judah if we try.

"We can firmly plant our faith in God, who will always do what is right."

Chapter 18 shows God as the potter. Jeremiah watched as the potter molded and fashioned the clay in his hand, and the Lord showed Jeremiah that He is the potter who molds His people in His own hands. Sometimes He has to change and rework the clay in order to make us more like Himself. God is sovereign over His children, and He will do what is best. We are the clay in the Master's hands, and we can trust Him to mold us into what we should be (Romans 9:20-21). We can firmly plant our faith in God, who will always do what is right.

QUESTIONS

Spend some time in self-examination in light of Jeremiah 16:12. What are some ways that we can resist following our own hearts and disobeying the Lord?

Focus on Jeremiah 17:9-10. What insight does this verse give you into understanding your own heart and mind?

Think about the analogy of the potter and the clay.
List out the ways that we are like clay and the Lord is like a potter.

Jeremiah 19-21

The Lord tells Jeremiah to buy a clay jar from a potter and go to the Ben Hinnom Valley and speak before the elders of the people and priests.

"We can rest securely in the eternal hope we have because of the gospel."

The Ben Hinnom Valley was known as a place for worship to the false god, Moloch. Child sacrifice was a common practice by worshipers of Moloch, and the altar where this would have happened was in this valley (2 Chronicles 28:1-3, Jeremiah 7:31). Jeremiah takes the clay jar to this horrible place and smashes it so that it is unmendable. He tells the people that the Lord will do the same to Judah. In the previous chapter, the Lord showed Jeremiah how He was the potter, and the people were His clay that He molded and changed. But now, the people are compared to a clay pot unable to be molded. The people of Judah were not moldable. They hardened their hearts against the Lord, and they allowed horrendous practices of idol worship and child sacrifice to persist. This destruction of human life was an abomination that goes against God's design for humans because God made people in His image. Human life is sacred, and human lives are valuable.

As Jeremiah prophesies this harsh reality, one of the leading priests, Pashhur, immediately beats and humiliates Jeremiah by placing him in the stocks to endure public shame. This would have signaled to the people that Jeremiah's message was false in the eyes of Judah's highest leaders. Even the priests, the men who represent the people to the Lord, ignored His word and allowed the Lord's name to be smeared by pagan worship. When Pashhur releases Jeremiah, the prophet does not lighten his message. He tells Pashhur the same message, but this time he specifically says that all of Judah will fall into the hands of Babylon, and Pashhur and his family will go into captivity. Pashhur and the other false priests and prophets will die in this foreign nation. The treatment of Jeremiah by the leading religious leaders should remind us of how Jesus will be beaten and humiliated by the Sanhedrin, the members of the ancient Jewish court system, before His death on the cross. A life lived in obedience to God is not easy, and we will experience suffering just as our Savior did, but we can rest securely in the eternal hope we have because of the gospel.

Jeremiah speaks to Judah's priests and kings when they have become worried over Nebuchadnezzar's advances against them. Jeremiah will confirm

that he is the king who will destroy Judah. Jeremiah also prophesies against the house of David because the kings of Judah had failed and were faithless. A foreign king, Nebuchadnezzar, would be temporarily allowed to overwhelm the nation. However, God would keep His promise to David. He would provide a faithful King, Jesus. Unlike the kings of old, Jesus will obey the Lord, fulfill the promises God made to David, and lead His people in righteousness (2 Samuel 7:8-17). Jesus will deliver His people from Babylon—the snares of sin—and let them return to the presence of God.

QUESTIONS

How does understanding the cultural context of the Ben Hinnom Valley change your understanding of Jeremiah 19?

Contrast Jeremiah 20:7-10 with Jeremiah 20:11-13. Why do you think there is such a stark change?

What does the warning in Jeremiah 21:8-14 teach you about God?

Jeremiah 22-24

In chapter 22, the Lord's message to the kings of Judah and house of David—which refers to David's lineage—continues.

Jeremiah goes to the king's house and tells him what the Lord has commanded him to do as the leader of God's chosen people: to act in justice and righteousness and to deliver the oppressed, which is the widow, the foreigner, and the orphan (Jeremiah 22:3). The Lord promised the king that if he were faithful to this command, the throne of David would continue to be filled with kings, but if the king disobeyed, the house would become "a ruin" (Jeremiah 22:5). The kings in the line of David had forsaken the Lord and His covenant with them. Because of this, they would be punished. And while the line of David would experience exile and hardship, it would not be destroyed. During Jeremiah's time, the wicked kings of Judah would be carried to exile in Babylon. They would die in this land and never return. But the Lord would raise a King who would obey the Lord's command and act righteously.

Jeremiah introduces us to this King, who is called the "Righteous Branch of David." He is the Shepherd King of Israel and Judah (Jeremiah 23:1-5). This King's name will mean, "The Lord is Our Righteousness" (Jeremiah 23:6). This King's name points to mankind's great need for righteousness, and the only One who could give them righteousness is the Lord. This is a prophecy that speaks directly about Jesus! The redeemed people of God will forever be in the care of Christ, the Righteous Branch and Shepherd King, who loves and cares for us. He will tenderly watch over us, and we will never be separated from Him. Jeremiah also goes strongly against the prophets of his day who were lying to the people and speaking messages contrary to God's Word. These prophets told the people that they would not go through the exile Jeremiah prophesied, but they were not proclaiming the truth. The Lord would be against these prophets because they put their words above the faithful, powerful Word of God. Their failure also points us to Jesus, who is our King and the greatest and last of the prophets. Jesus is called the last prophet, not because He is simply a prophet, but because He is the last person God speaks through. Jesus fulfills the prophets' messages because He is the Word of God in the flesh. He will not speak deceitful messages. He will speak what His Father instructs Him to say (John 12:49).

"Jesus fulfills the prophets' messages because He is the Word of God in the flesh."

In Jeremiah 24, the exile that Jeremiah has proclaimed comes to fruition. The son of Judah's king, Jeconiah, has been taken into captivity along with other important officials and tradesmen. The Lord gives Jeremiah another word picture to encourage the faithful remnant from Judah. The Lord shows Jeremiah a basket containing both ripe and rotten figs. The ripe figs are the faithful remnant of people. These figs will go into captivity, but they will return. The Lord will give them new hearts to know and love Him. The rotten figs represent those in Judah who have rejected God. They will be destroyed. This new heart the Lord describes foreshadows the coming new covenant, which is the new agreement we have with God. In this new agreement, everyone who believes in the death and resurrection of Christ will be given a new heart and united to God.

QUESTIONS

Reflect on Jeremiah 22 and Exodus 34. How do the verses in Exodus help you to understand the covenant that Israel has grievously broken?

Meditate on Jeremiah 23:5-6. How does this passage spark hope within you?

Reread Jeremiah 24:4-7. Think about the magnitude of this statement in light of the destruction and discipline that God's people have faced. Why do you think this is such a powerful verse?

Jeremiah 25-27

For 23 years, Jeremiah gave God's Word to the people. But the people rejected Jeremiah's message again and again.

"God is sovereign, and in His sovereignty, He can use anyone to accomplish His purposes."

The Lord had urged His people to return. They had received plenty of time to repent and come back to Him before His judgment. He had given them every opportunity, but their hearts were hardened. Now the Lord would send Nebuchadnezzar against them. He even refers to Nebuchadnezzar, a pagan king, as His servant. Judah's surviving people would be in Babylon for seventy years, and then the faithful remnant of Judah would return, and God would turn His judgment on Nebuchadnezzar and all of the nations who had rejected Him. They would drink from the cup of God's wrath. Christ would later use the imagery of God's cup of wrath before He suffered on the cross (Matthew 26:37-39). What is important for us to understand about Jesus's death is that while crucifixion would be a horrible way to die, it was not the main cause of Christ's suffering. What made Jesus's death infinitely worse was that He took on the full wrath of God for all the sins of His chosen people. He took on the sins of the people past, present, and to come.

The Lord sends Jeremiah to prophesy inside the temple courts to all the cities of Judah and everyone who came to the temple to worship Him. Though the people of Judah carried on with temple festivities, their hearts were far from Him. Their worship and sacrifices were hollow and empty. The Lord tells Jeremiah to declare to the people that if they do not listen, the temple will become like Shiloh, and Jerusalem, the city of God, would become a curse. When God says that He will make the temple like Shiloh, He is referring to when the Philistines conquered the city and carried off the ark of the covenant (1 Samuel 4). The priests and temple leaders are angry and want to kill Jeremiah for this message, but when the ruling princes and elders of Judah heard His message, they prevented his execution and told the priests it would be wise to heed Jeremiah's warning. When Jesus speaks among the people during His earthly ministry, He will cause the same kind of stir among the religious leaders. And when He goes to the temple and righteously clears it of unholy practices, the religious leaders will seek to kill Him just like their ancestors sought to kill Jeremiah. Jesus is the fulfillment of the prophets' prophecies.

God is sovereign, and in His sovereignty, He can use anyone to accomplish His purposes, even Nebuchadnezzar. And God would send Jeremiah to deliver His message that commanded Judah and the surrounding nations to submit to Nebuchadnezzar's rule. Jeremiah would wear an actual yoke before the king of Judah, who at the time was conspiring with other nations against Babylon, to remind him that Nebuchadnezzar was who the Lord had chosen to rule over them. The Lord would eventually bring His faithful remnant back to Jerusalem, and the promise of the Messiah would continue, even in such a seemingly hopeless situation.

QUESTIONS

Reread Jeremiah 25:7. How does this verse convey some of the effects that sin has on our lives?

What reasons do you see for why the priests and the people of Judah seized Jeremiah in 26:7-11? Do we tend to hate correction and rebuke as well? Why might it be important to recognize these same tendencies in our own lives?

Focus on Jeremiah 27:22. How does this show us how the Lord handles sin? In what ways is this both a warning to us and a message of hope?

Jeremiah 28-30

When we read prophetic words in the Old Testament, we might think that those prophets were the only people speaking messages from the Lord.

The reality was that there were many prophets, and Scripture only gives us a glimpse into the messages and lives of the few who are most important for understanding God's redemptive story. However, while other true prophets lived outside of the ones we read about in our Bibles, there were many more false prophets who tried to lead the people astray. Jeremiah 28 gives us an example of one such prophet: Hananiah.

Hananiah told Judah that they would only be in exile in Babylon for two years. However, the Lord had already spoken through Jeremiah and said they would be there for seventy. Hananiah was speaking a message that would have appealed greatly to the people. It was what they wanted to hear. He was so confident in his message that he took the yoke Jeremiah was still symbolically wearing and smashed it. But just because Hananiah was passionate about his message did not make it true. The Lord would put Hananiah to death that very year because of his false messages, and He would tell Hananiah that the yoke He was putting on Judah would be one of iron. It was "unsmashable." Looking now to the New Testament, one of Jesus's final warnings is against false prophets and false messiahs (Matthew 24:23-28). This is why we must carefully compare the teachings of men to the Word of God, and we must also take care not to believe messages that appeal to the ease and pleasure of the world and not the way of Jesus.

The people of Judah would go to exile, but Jeremiah would bring a message that they must move forward in the place they found themselves. Babylon would be their new home, and their lives must continue (Jeremiah 29:4-9). Judah's faithful remnant must marry and have children because it will be through their line that the Messiah will come. They were not to live begrudgingly in Babylon. Instead, they were to pray for its welfare. While many false prophets would try and convince Judah of messages other than what the Lord had spoken through Jeremiah, they were not to listen. The Lord had good plans for them, and He would redeem their brokenness and pain. Their future and hope were secure in Him.

"He is our perfect Prophet, Priest, and King."

Chapter 30 turns to a promise of their final restoration. Though the promises in this passage point to the future, it would remind God's people and us of who He is and what is to come in Jesus. He is our perfect Prophet, Priest, and King. The Lord intended to use this exile to discipline Judah for their sin, but He promised that He was always with them to save them (Jeremiah 30:11). God would deliver them, heal them, and bring peace. The rescue from Babylon foreshadows the day when Jesus will bring perfect peace to His people once and for all.

QUESTIONS

In chapter 28, we see a continuation of the imagery and symbolism of the "yoke." What do you think the message of this illustration is?

Summarize Jeremiah's letter to the exiles in 29:4-29 in your own words.

Meditate on Jeremiah 30:18-22. How does this verse tell us more about who Jesus is?

Jeremiah 31-33

The Lord continues to speak of the restoration that He will bring to His faithful remnant in Jeremiah 31.

He tells them that He has loved them with an everlasting love and that He has been faithful to them. This everlasting love and faithfulness are available to everyone who is in Christ. No matter the trial or difficulty we face in this world, nothing can separate us from the love of Jesus. The Lord continues to give promises of hope and healing to His people. One day, He will bring each one of the faithful of Judah back to their home after they have been exiled (Jeremiah 31:7-9). This return also points us to when all of the faithful, including those who believe in Christ, will live with God in eternity. The words that the Lord uses to describe how He will care for His people remind us of Christ, our tender Shepherd King, who will care for us by ransoming our lives by shedding His blood. The astounding language at the end of this passage is the basis for our new covenant in Christ, and it is referenced many times throughout the New Testament. In Christ, we receive new hearts that have God's law written on them, and we will be saved from our sin. We will know God!

In chapter 32, Jeremiah is in prison because King Zedekiah is frustrated with Jeremiah's prophecies of judgment. Nebuchadnezzar is besieging Jerusalem, and Jeremiah knows that it is only a matter of time before the city comes under his control as God has promised. However, God gives him a strange task. He tells Jeremiah to buy a field from his cousin in Judah. Jeremiah must have been taken aback by the Lord's request. All of Judah was about to be razed and controlled by the Babylonians. Now was hardly the time to make a real estate investment. Jeremiah prays to the Lord. In his prayer, he praises God, recalls His wonderful works, and then he asks the Lord why he needs to buy the field. And the Lord responds that though Babylon may seem to be victorious right now, the Lord would bring His people back to their home. Jeremiah could buy the field in confidence, knowing that the redeemed people of God would someday return and possess the land. The Lord rejoices in bringing His people home and doing them good. We must remember this as we wander this world before reaching our final home with Christ. The Lord will delight in bringing us home to Him when our time on earth is complete.

"The Lord will delight in bringing us home to Him when our time on earth is complete."

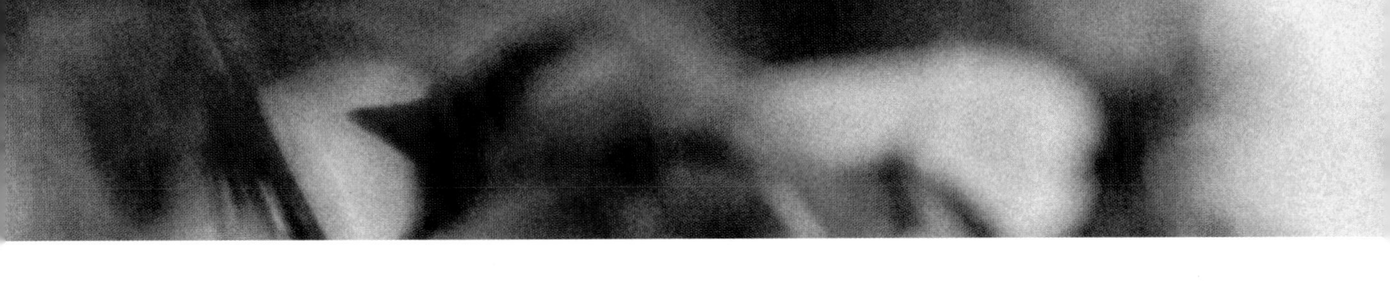

The beautiful promises of the Lord to His people continue in chapter 33. The Lord will cleanse His people from their sin, and He will remove evil from His city. Even though they would endure hardship throughout the exile, it would ultimately be used for their good. Jerusalem would no longer be like all the other nations filled with horrible practices like child sacrifice and idol worship. Instead, God would make it a place of joy and glory. This renewal is what the Lord does for our hearts through the gospel. The Lord promises the remnant of Judah His Righteous Branch again, which we know is another name for Christ (Jeremiah 33:15). This Righteous Branch will fulfill God's promise to David (2 Samuel 7:8-17), and He will give Jerusalem His name, thus acting as their mediator. Christ will also give us His name by placing His righteousness on us.

QUESTIONS

Think about the love of God spoken about in Jeremiah 31:3. In what ways have you seen God's faithful love expressed in your life?

Reread Jeremiah 32:39-41. What does integrity of heart and action look like?

Focus on Jeremiah 33:2-3. Why do you think that the Lord introduces Himself the way that He does in verse 2?

Jeremiah 34-36

The Lord continues to show undeserved mercy to Zedekiah and Judah as Nebuchadnezzar and all his kingdoms besieged the city.

Zedekiah—out of fear—tried to rebel against the Lord's decrees by turning against Babylon instead of surrendering to them. Even so, the Lord tells Zedekiah that he will die in peace if he obeys Him. But Zedekiah shows that he is faithless again and again. For example, he promised the slaves of Judah they could go free, but he did not keep his word. By doing so, Zedekiah broke the Lord's command that required the people of Israel to release their slaves every seven years (Jeremiah 34:14). He was not a righteous king, and he did not care for the poor or the oppressed, which were the very people God sought to protect. The Lord promises Zedekiah that he and anyone else who wrongly kept their slaves would be severely punished. God delights in freeing His people. He had freed Israel from slavery many years ago, and now His own people were wrongfully doing what the Egyptians had done to them. Hundreds of years later, God would send a new king, Jesus. Jesus will not be a king like Zedekiah, and He will reign in righteousness and justice. Slaves are liberated under Christ, both spiritually and physically.

In chapter 35, Judah is contrasted with the Rechabites. The Rechabites were a radical sect of Israelites who lived in the wilderness and tried to pattern their lives after Israel's early nomads. They lived simple lives in tents and shepherded their flocks. One of their ancestors, Jonadab, commanded them not to drink wine and live simply to avoid idolatry and sin. For generations, they listened to this command and obeyed. The Rechabites were faithful, and the Lord uses their testimony as an example of what He wants His people to be like. He desired their faithful obedience. He wanted them to honor Him as their Father, like the Rechabites honored their ancestors. And the Lord desires this same faithfulness from us. He has saved us through the blood of Christ, and as we grow to know Him more and more, we will desire to obey Him. Our obedience is an act of worship and love toward God, our great Father.

In Jeremiah 36, we learn that Jeremiah has a scribe named Baruch who writes down everything Jeremiah says. The Lord tells Jeremiah to put all of the words He has spoken to him in a scroll and then read it to the people of Judah. Jeremiah sends the scroll with Baruch to read in the temple since Jeremiah has been banned from entering. As the people listen to Jeremiah's prophecies, one godly man, Micaiah, hears the words and trembles. He quickly tells the princes

"Truly, no one can thwart God's plans."

of Judah about the prophecies, and they send for Baruch. Baruch reads the scroll to them, and they are also greatly troubled. They take the scroll and tell Baruch and Jeremiah to hide because they are going to read it to the king, and he will not be pleased. King Jehoiakim hears the scroll and burns it piece by piece. He is not afraid of the words at all. He despises them. Just as Jesus is unlike Zedekiah, He is also unlike Jehoiakim. He follows every word the Lord says because He is the incarnate Word of God, which means that He is the Word of God in human form. And as Jehoiakim could not thwart the Word of God by burning it, the incarnate Word of God will not be thwarted by those who seek to take His life. Instead, Jesus fulfills God's law, bears our sin, dies on the cross, and rises on the third day to pay the penalty of sin once and for all. Truly, no one can thwart God's plans.

QUESTIONS

Meditate on Jeremiah 35:15. Is it easy for you to pay attention to those who are speaking truth into your life? How does the book of Jeremiah express to you the importance of listening to the truth being spoken into our lives, even if we do not like it?

Reflect on Jeremiah 34:14. Why do you think that it was important to God that slaves be released every seven years. What does this tell you about God's mercy, even in the Old Testament?

From reading the book of Jeremiah, why is it so important to listen to rebuke from other believers?

Jeremiah 37-39

In the last few chapters, Jeremiah switches between the kings of Judah rather frequently.

Most commentators agree that Jeremiah is not necessarily putting these prophecies in chronological order. He may even be recalling them as he speaks to King Zedekiah before Judah's final fall. At the beginning of chapter 37, we are taken back to when Zedekiah first becomes king. The Chaldeans had started to attack Jerusalem, and Zedekiah pleaded with Jeremiah to intercede to the Lord. When the Egyptian army distracts the Chaldeans away from the city, Jeremiah warns Zedekiah that destruction is coming. Soon after, Jeremiah is imprisoned falsely for his harsh words against Judah, but when Zedekiah takes him out of imprisonment to question him again, Jeremiah's answer does not change. Jeremiah and Zedekiah's interaction is a picture of the interactions between the Lord and Judah. The Lord wanted His people to obey Him, but they rejected His Word again.

Zedekiah goes so far as to allow leading officials to throw Jeremiah into a cistern and leaving him to die. And when Jeremiah is saved, it is not because the king seeks him out to repent or hear from God; it is because an Ethiopian eunuch approaches the king and asks for Jeremiah's deliverance from the cistern. The eunuch, a Gentile, knew that Jeremiah was a man of God, and he feared the Lord and wanted to save Jeremiah because of that. Once Jeremiah was free, Zedekiah seeks him out again, just in case the Word of God has changed. And God is still merciful and offers Zedekiah another chance to repent and surrender on behalf of himself, his household, and the entire city. But we learn in chapter 39 that he does not.

The Babylonians finally besiege Jerusalem, and though Zedekiah and his family try to escape, they are chased down and brought before Nebuchadnezzar. The last thing Zedekiah sees is the murder of his children and companions, and then his eyes are gouged out. His disobedience and hardness of heart have led to destruction. Zedekiah's life and downfall remind us of the most important question every human being must answer: do we surrender to Christ, or do we refuse to do so? Surrendering to Him leads to eternal peace and life, but refusing to surrender leads to death. And while Zedekiah never repented and

"Surrendering to Him leads to eternal peace and life."

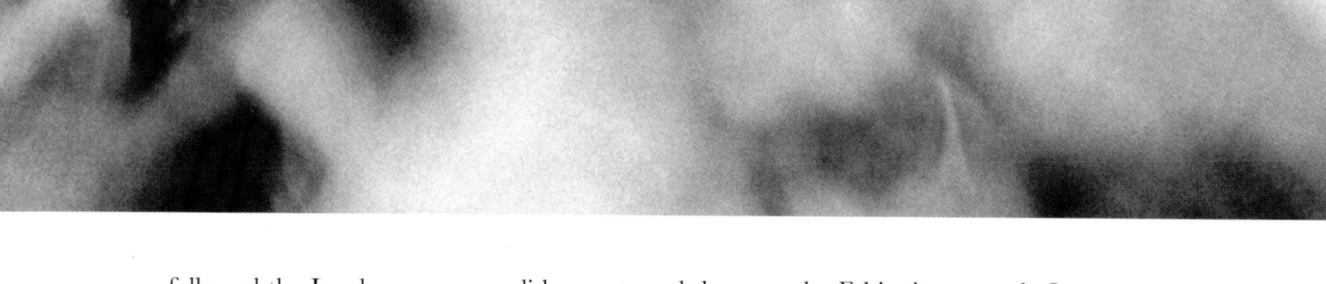

followed the Lord, one person did repent, and that was the Ethiopian eunuch. It was not the king of Judah who feared God, but a Gentile man whose condition was condemned by Levitical law, which is the law given in the book of Leviticus. Because the eunuch followed God, God delivered him. And, He offers this deliverance to all of those who love Him.

QUESTIONS

How does Jeremiah's response to opposition in chapter 37 teach you about faithfulness to God?

What does chapter 38 reveal about God's plan versus the enemy's plan?

In your own words, how would you describe the sequence of events in chapters 37-39?

Jeremiah 40-42

As the city of Jerusalem is burned and destroyed, the Babylonians gather up many people to take them into exile, just as the Lord had promised.

Jeremiah is collected with them, but Nebuzaradan, the captain of the guard, releases him soon after his capture. As Nebuzaradan speaks to Jeremiah, it is obvious that he has heard and listened to Jeremiah's prophecies. Nebuzaradan knew that Jerusalem had fallen because of the people's disobedience to the Lord. His belief in Jeremiah's prophecies was stronger than the belief of the people of Judah. The captain of the guard gives Jeremiah a choice to go to Babylon or stay in Judah, and if he chooses to go to Babylon, the captain says he will take care of him. It is obvious that the Lord is showing Jeremiah He will provide for and take care of him. And even though Jeremiah could have experienced a life of ease and comfort in Babylon, he chose to stay in Judah's war-torn land because He believed God's promises were true and knew that one day all of Judah's faithful remnant would return to the land. Jeremiah was consistently obedient to the Lord, and his obedience reminds us of Christ's obedience to the Father. Jesus will give up the ease and pleasure of the world to fulfill the mission for which He was sent.

The Babylonians leave a faithful man, Gedaliah, in charge of Judah, but jealousy and bitterness from neighboring kingdoms lead to his murder. Worst of all, he is murdered at the hand of a friend and fellow Israelite, Ishmael (Jeremiah 41:1-3). Ishmael will go on to kill and plumage innocent people after Gedaliah's death. The events following Jerusalem's fall show a descent into chaos and the result of rebellion against the Word of God. Gedaliah tried to lead the people to submit to what God decreed through Jeremiah, but Ishmael's murderous ways caused Gedaliah's plan to all fall apart. Though the people left in Judah would be rescued from Ishmael, Gedaliah's death and Ishmael's insurrection were just another reminder that the Messiah God had promised had not yet come. Jesus is the only one who will bring order out of chaos, and He will lead His people in righteousness and perfectly restore them from their sin. Even though He will also be murdered at the hands of wicked men, death will not hold Him, and He will reign forever (Acts 2:24).

The people of Judah are finally rescued from Ishmael by a man named Johanan and his armed forces (Jeremiah 41:11-18). Afterward, they approached Jeremiah and asked for guidance about where they should go and what they

"He will never stop being faithful to us."

should do. They told him they would obey whatever the Lord said. However, as we will see in Jeremiah 43, their minds were already made up. The Lord was clear that the people were to stay in the land and that He would protect them. He was firm that they were not to go back to Egypt, as this had been a place for them to turn to instead of trusting in Him. As far back as Abraham, God's people tended to run to Egypt when they were worried instead of running to the Lord. Yet the Lord promised them He would be faithful right where He had called them to be. We must remind our hearts of the same truth. We do not need to run to the world for comfort and protection. Instead, we must run to our God, who is the one who will guide and protect us right where He has called us to be. He will never stop being faithful to us.

QUESTIONS

How does the Babylonians' understanding of the Lord's plan in Jeremiah 40:1-6 contrast with Judah's?

Meditate on Jeremiah 42:5-6. What does this response teach us about complete obedience in light of the full passage?

Think back to the entire history of Israel and Judah that we saw in Ezra and Nehemiah. How is the Lord's promise in Jeremiah 42:10 fulfilled?

Jeremiah 43-45

After delivering the warning of the Lord to the people, telling them not to go to Egypt and put their trust in foreign nations instead of Him, the people accuse Jeremiah of lying.

It is incredible to read that after seeing Jeremiah's prophecies regarding the destruction and fall of Judah come to fruition, that the people still reject him and question his truthfulness. Instead of listening to Jeremiah, Judah ignores the Lord's words again, and they go to Egypt. Johanan and the other leading men heartbreakingly take Jeremiah to Egypt against his will. This must have been one of the saddest moments of his life. Jeremiah had prophesied for most of his life about how God would be faithful to bring His people back home to the land He had given them, and he was forced to leave. The lives of the people of God do not always have a happy ending in the eyes of the world, but their future is set in eternity. When Judah arrives in Egypt, Jeremiah tells them that Nebuchadnezzar would soon come to conquer them and bring destruction. The people put false hope into a nation that could not save them. Similarly, we put our hope in the empty things of this world when all of our hope should be placed in Christ. He is the only one who can save us. The things of this world will fail us, but He has provided us eternal security through His blood (Acts 20:28).

In Jeremiah 44, the prophet speaks directly to Judah about their idolatrous behavior against the Lord. Judah continued to do the same things they did before its destruction. They have not learned how serious it is to worship gods other than the Lord, and the Lord promises that the destruction they saw in Jerusalem would happen again in Egypt. The people who went there to seek refuge and continued in idol worship would face destruction as well. However, not all of Judah would be destroyed, and there would be yet another remnant of Judah who would escape. Yet again, Judah is not affected by these words and continues to brazenly worship other gods. Like Judah, we also worship other gods. Though we do not worship idols set up on physical altars, we often worship other idols that are harder to spot: wealth, appearance, safety, freedom, family, etc. None of these things are bad, but if we put all of our trust in them instead of the Lord, they are indeed idols in our lives. Christ lived a life free of idolatry. He sought God and depended on Him in every circumstance and situation, and because we are united with Christ, He will help us recognize idolatry in our lives and choose the better way.

"We can trust in our eternal hope."

Jeremiah 45 gives us a short look into the life of Baruch, Jeremiah's scribe. Writing down all of the prophetic messages for Jeremiah was a heavy task, and we see the weight that he felt in this passage. We know from previous chapters that the people blamed Baruch for Jeremiah's prophecy that spoke against them going to Egypt. And yet, the Lord tells Baruch that even though destruction surrounds him, He will deliver him. The Lord reminds Baruch not to seek great things for himself but to remember what God has promised to Him. Jesus gives a similar message to those who follow Him. We are challenged to set our minds on heaven and the glory of God instead of ourselves. We can trust in our eternal hope.

QUESTIONS

What does the response of the people in Jeremiah 43:2 reveal to you about the deception of sin?

Reread Jeremiah 44:10. What does this show you about the connection between humility and obedience?

Paraphrase Jeremiah 45 in your own words.

Jeremiah 46-48

In Jeremiah 46 to 51, the Lord gives a series of judgments to foreign nations outside of Judah.

The first four chapters of these judgments address several different nations that surrounded Judah. The last two chapters are specifically for the nation of Babylon. The judgments pronounced in these chapters are horrific, and while these days of destruction were severe, they are only a shadow of the coming judgment that will happen when Jesus returns to earth to destroy evil once and for all (Revelation 20:11-15). The Lord repeats patterns so that people will recognize the truth, repent, and turn to Him. Even Judah's destruction was so that the nations would see He is one, true God. It is important to remember as we read these chapters that no human being, besides Jesus, is innocent. Every single human being is sinful, and we are all deserving of God's wrath. The judgment is written in these chapters is the judgment we deserve, and yet, Jesus stood in our place. He took our sin so that we could be washed and covered in His righteousness.

Turning back to the book of Jeremiah, the Lord pronounces judgment on Egypt first, which makes sense since He has just spoken to His people of the destruction that is coming there. At the end of the judgment, the Lord gives His faithful remnant of people hope. Though they fled to the land that had once held their ancestors captive, the Lord would deliver them again. They would face discipline for their sin against Him, but He would not completely destroy them. Their fate would be unlike the other nations surrounding them. Their ancient enemies, the Philistines, and their wandering cousins and neighbors, the Moabites, would be completely overcome by Babylon. Even though some of the Moabites would be allowed to return from captivity, the nation would never return to what it once was.

The Lord does not delight in pouring out this judgment on the nations, but the sin they committed was grievous, and they had no desire to repent. We must remember that the nation of Israel had been among the Philistines and Moabites for generations. God had given these foreign nations every opportunity to repent and turn to Him as they observed His chosen people, but they refused. The Lord sends us out to the nations, just as He sent out Israel. And though many will reject the truth of the gospel, there will be those who will have hearts softened by the Lord and believe. Judgment is coming, but salvation has been given in Christ!

"Judgment is coming, but salvation has been given in Christ!"

QUESTIONS

What hope do you see for Israel in Jeremiah 46?

What do the prophecies against Judah's surrounding peoples reveal to you about God's justice?

What other aspects of God's character do these chapters reveal?

Jeremiah 49-52

In Jeremiah 49, the Lord gives judgments to multiple nations.

While some are told they will one day see restoration, others are not. They will be destroyed. One of the most notable is the nation of Edom, the descendants of Esau. Throughout the Bible, the Edomites represent those who will never believe in God. This means that people who do not believe in God will meet a similar ending to the people of Edom.

The harshest of all the judgments by far is reserved for Babylon, the nation that carried out many of the judgments God decreed. They will face punishment for coming up against God's people and burning down His temple. The Lord will go to war against them, and they will be humbled. Cyrus, the king of Persia, will be God's chosen instrument who fulfills what the Lord promises to this nation. God's judgment of the Babylonians is significant because they represent all evil. This judgment foreshadows the final judgment Jesus will bring when He returns to earth. The destruction of Babylon will be sudden and swift, which reminds us of the New Testament's language describing the last days, which will come like "a thief in the night" (1 Thessalonians 5:2). Only the Lord knows the time and day Jesus will return.

In Jeremiah 51, the Lord gives us an incredible description of who He is and how Babylon, a mighty nation of great conquerors, is nothing compared to Him. Babylon may seem mighty according to the wisdom of the world. However, godly wisdom knows and recognizes that the Lord is above all. He will always defend His chosen people. In the eyes of the world, the gospel is foolishness. But to the godly, it is the true source of wisdom. The strongest evil the world holds may seem like it may win, but we know that Jesus is victorious. He will defeat all evil forever, and He will lead His people back to Zion, the eternal city of God (Romans 11:26). Nebuchadnezzar may have burned the grand and glorious temple Solomon built for the Lord, and even though they would rebuild a second temple, a temple would soon no longer be necessary. Jesus gives us access to the Lord, and He dwells in our hearts through the Holy Spirit. When the entire faithful remnant of Israel returns to the Lord, we will physically dwell with Him. Jeremiah shows us God's judgment for His people, but it is not without hope!

"Jesus gives us access to the Lord, and He dwells in our hearts through the Holy Spirit."

QUESTIONS

How are the promises of God contrasted positively and negatively in these chapters according to the people's responses?

Compare and contrast Jerusalem and Babylon.

Now that we have finished reading Jeremiah, what are the most prominent things you have learned?

Lord, bring
us back
to yourself.

Lamentations

GENRE: *Prophet, Poetry*

AUTHOR / DATE WRITTEN

Unknown, likely Jeremiah • c. 586 BC

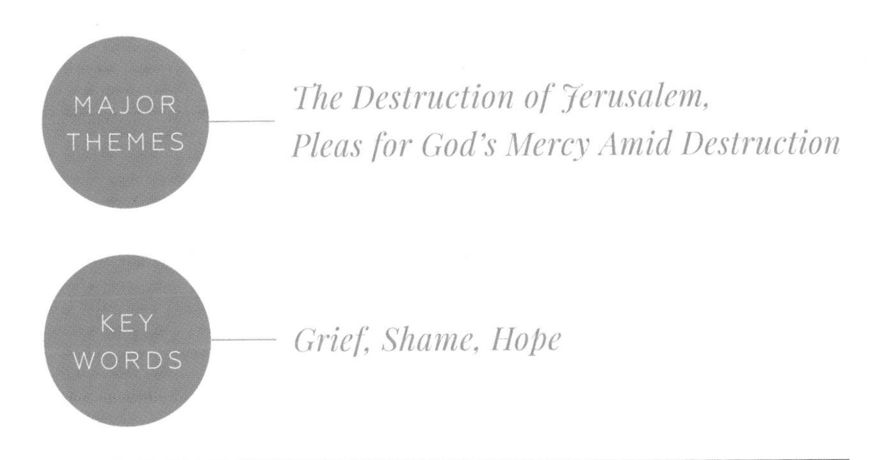

MAJOR THEMES — *The Destruction of Jerusalem, Pleas for God's Mercy Amid Destruction*

KEY WORDS — *Grief, Shame, Hope*

KEY VERSES

LAMENTATIONS 5:21-22

Lord, bring us back to yourself, so we may return; renew our days as in former times, unless you have completely rejected us and are intensely angry with us.

Lamentations 1-3

Lamentations is a book of poetry written after the fall of Jerusalem.

There are five poems in acrostic form, which means that certain letters in each line form a word. In this case, each verse begins with a letter of the Hebrew alphabet in successive order. This pattern is broken in the fifth poem. However, there are still 22 verses—each verse representing a letter of the Hebrew alphabet. This shows us that the author of Lamentations is covering the topic of suffering as much as he can. Though the author of Lamentations is unknown, many commentators attribute it as being written by Jeremiah. Jeremiah grieved over Judah's rejection of the Lord, and he wept over the destruction of the cherished city of Jerusalem. God's people had too many "lovers" instead of clinging to their true love, the Lord. They rejected their covenant with their faithful God for unfaithful companions who would leave them. As a result, the city of Jerusalem was destroyed because of their sins. The first poem describes Jerusalem as a woman who sits in shame and nakedness. The state of Jerusalem reminds us of the natural consequences of sin and rebellion against God. It also foreshadows the grief and suffering that Jesus will bear for us on the cross as He takes on the sins of the people of God. He, too, will face rejection from the Lord, but because He conquered sin, He can bring all the people of God back to their eternal home in Zion. The city Jeremiah describes will not be sad forever. It will be restored at the end of days in Christ.

The immense grief and sorrow Jeremiah feels over the destruction of the city of Jerusalem is different from times when the people have suffered before. This time, the destruction of Jerusalem was not accomplished by a foreign enemy alone. God used Babylon as His agent of discipline and judgment against His own people. There is nothing more terrifying than facing God's wrath. Chapter 2 provides detail after detail about how the Lord has come against Judah, and this in itself causes us to cry out to Jesus in thanksgiving for what He has done on our behalf. The wrath described in this chapter is what we deserved, but Jesus stood in our place. Yet, we still need to mourn over our sin and the havoc it causes. Before we are saved, it has caused a separation between God and us. But God does the unthinkable through the gospel. While He could become a warrior against us, He acts as our Redeemer and saves us from ourselves. He is gracious above measure.

"We are covered in the faithfulness and mercy of God."

Chapter 3 of Lamentations is the center of the book, and it is the focal point of the author's message. Jeremiah spends the first two poems deeply lamenting Judah's sins, and in the third poem, he actually begins by taking on the weight of Judah's sin. His language foreshadows Christ as the Suffering Servant on our behalf. After this, Jeremiah does what we must do as well. He remembers who God is, and He finds hope in God alone. He found confidence and hope in the unchanging character of our God who never changes. His mercies are new every day, and His faithfulness never fails (Lamentations 3:22-23). We must do the same. While grief over sin is a healthy practice in the believer's life, we are covered in the faithfulness and mercy of God. This is the hope that allows us to press on. God redeems us!

QUESTIONS

Look up the word "lament" or "lamentation" in the dictionary. How does this definition help give you an idea about what this book will be like?

After reading chapters 1 and 2 and seeing the way that the prophet describes his beloved people and nation, spend some time in reflection. How does this chapter convey the deep effects of sin?

Meditate on Lamentations 3:32-33. What does this teach you about God? How does this deepen your understanding of suffering?

Lamentations 4-5

The lamentation in chapter 4 reminds us how the people of Judah had given up everything to go their own way.

For generations, the Lord loved and protected His chosen people. He called them in the time of Abraham, delivered them from the bondage of Egypt, and brought them into the Promised Land. He had been with them every step of the way, and yet they turned away from His love. He had never broken His promise, yet they tossed it aside. The world looked at Israel and saw them as untouchable because the Lord was on their side. They believed this as well, but they were not untouchable to the Lord. He was the only one who would allow true and lasting destruction to fall on them by His hand. The effect of this destruction is detailed throughout the fourth poem, and it is heartbreaking. The nation of Judah had fallen into chaos and disorder. Yet, God gives hope to His people by telling them that their destruction has been "accomplished." It would not go on forever. This foreshadows the accomplishment of Christ on the cross. When He says that it is finished as He takes His last breath and then resurrects from the dead three days later, the world sighs in relief. The curse of sin has been conquered, and while we still feel its presence from day to day, it does not control us anymore. We are made into new creations in Christ.

Chapter 5 contains a prayer from Jeremiah as he pleads with the Lord to remember His own. Though chastening was necessary, the Lord would never once forget His own. The situation was bleak, but Jeremiah and the remnant of God's people could see His glory shine through, even in captivity. It would be seventy years until the captivity ended, and yet even in captivity, the Lord was faithful. This final poem reminds us of the state of the world. Each day we see how sin has taken its toll on the world around us, and we wonder when it will end. Like Jeremiah, we can cry out, "Restore us, O Lord," and we can know that He will! When we are in Christ, sin no longer separates us from the Lord, even though we experience sanctification until the day we die. One day, when Christ returns to earth, the Lord will restore all things, and we will be with Him forever. Lamenting over sin will cease, and there will only be rejoicing over the Lord's graciousness and mercy.

"We are made into new creations in Christ."

QUESTIONS

Focus on Lamentations 4:22. How does this verse expand your understanding of the consequences of sin? How does this teach you not to be arrogant in thinking your sins will always remain hidden without repentance?

Summarize the prayer of chapter 5 in your own words.

Now that you have finished reading the book of Lamentations, what are some of the most prominent themes you have found?

I will give
you a
new heart.

Ezekiel

GENRE: *Prophet, Exilic*

AUTHOR / DATE WRITTEN

Ezekiel • c. 593-565 BC

The Dwelling Place for the Glory of the Lord, Faithfulness of God in Exile

Temple, Exile, Restoration

KEY VERSE

EZEKIEL 36:26

I will give you a new heart and put a new spirit within you; I will remove your heart of stone and give you a heart of flesh.

Ezekiel 1-3

The book of Ezekiel begins with the Word of the Lord coming to Ezekiel when he was among the exiled people in Babylon.

Already, this is a beautiful reminder that the Lord has not forgotten His people in Babylon. The book begins with Ezekiel sitting by a canal. As he sits, he sees a stormy wind approach him and then clouds and fire all around it. It opens, and through the center, the attendants of the Lord—the cherubim—begin to appear. As the vision continues, he begins to see divine wheels full of eyes moving all about. Ezekiel is seeing the divine chariot of the Lord. This symbolizes how God is going to war. Then Ezekiel sees the throne of God and One taking the form of a man is sitting upon it. This beautiful picture of the glory of the Lord is also an example of the preincarnate Christ. The term "preincarnate Christ" means that this is Christ before he took on the form of man as documented in the New Testament. Ezekiel is seeing the Savior of the world who is yet to humble Himself from His heavenly position and take on flesh. Jesus truly is throughout the Old Testament.

As Ezekiel stands stunned by what He is seeing, the Lord calls out to Him and tells Him that He has called Him to speak. However, Ezekiel will not be free to say whatever he wishes, he will only say the words the Lord gives Him. The Lord puts His Spirit inside Ezekiel, just as He will one day put His Spirit inside of us. The preincarnate Christ, the Word of God, gives Ezekiel His own Words in the form of a scroll to bring to the people of Israel. And as people reject Christ's words in the New Testament, they reject the messages that Ezekiel brings.

In chapter 3, the Lord commands Ezekiel to eat the scroll, and he does. The scroll is as sweet to him as honey. This represents how the Word of God is our daily food. It sustains us and helps us grow. It is both sweet and bitter. It is sweet with encouragement and life-giving truth, and it is bitter with conviction and instruction. We soon discover that Israel wanted only the feel-good words from false prophets instead of the life-giving words of God. God was sending Ezekiel as a watchman for Israel to warn them of their rebellion and sin. If they rejected Ezekiel's words, they would be rejecting the Lord's words. When Jesus comes to earth, He speaks the life-giving message of salvation. To reject Christ's words is the same as rejecting the Word of God. We must run to the Lord and take in all He has for us. His words give life!

"We must run to the Lord and take in all He has for us."

QUESTIONS

Meditate on all of chapter 1. How does this chapter give you a better understanding of the Lord's glory?

2. Reread Ezekiel 1:28. Why did Ezekiel fall facedown at the sound of the Lord's voice? Why is this significant?

3. What does chapter 3 teach you about the importance of God's Word and the importance of obeying the instruction of the Lord?

Ezekiel 4-6

God extended so much mercy on His chosen people, but there would be consequences for their rejection of the Lord.

The hearts of the people of Judah were hardened to the truth, so Ezekiel uses action sermons instead of words. He acted out his messages to the people and showed them the calamity they faced from God's hand. They had turned from His mercy and were facing His judgment. One of the first actions the Lord commands Ezekiel to take is to create a miniature model of the city with tiny platforms around it, representing the siege of Jerusalem the Lord had promised. Ezekiel would then lay bound on his side, facing away from the city, with a cooking grate between him and the tiny model. Ezekiel represents the Lord's decision to bring judgment upon His people, and the cooking grate represents the finality of what He decided to do. Ezekiel would lay there for 490 days, and the food he ate while doing so was very scarce. He would even cook it over cow dung to further represent the sinfulness of the people and how they had made themselves unclean (Ezekiel 4:15). The scenes in Ezekiel are not the only time we will see God turn away from His people. In Matthew 27:46, we will see God turn away from Jesus as Jesus bears our sin on the cross. Jesus took our filth and shamefulness and covered us with His righteousness.

And yet, even in the message of the coming judgment was a promise that God's mercy would save a remnant of Israel. Ezekiel shows this in chapter 5 when he shaves his head to symbolize what the nation was facing. A third of his hair he burned because a third of Judah would die as the city burned to the ground. A third of his hair he cut with a sword because a third of the people would die at the Babylonians' hands. But the remaining third of his hair he carefully tucked into the hem of his garment as a reminder that God would save some of the people and allow them to one day return to their homeland. God's faithful remnant of people would be spared, just as He promised, and eventually, He would bring the Messiah out of Judah. God never breaks His promises.

"Jesus took our filth and shamefulness and covered us with His righteousness."

However, before the remnant of Israel can be saved, we will see how Israel's idolatry will bring about their destruction. In Ezekiel 6, the Lord promises them that the spiritual death caused by idol worship would become a physical reality. The bones of those who had worshiped idols in Judah would be laid before the idols' altars after the destruction of the city. The land would be purged of evil by the sword, disease, and famine, and those who had rejected the Lord and worshiped false gods would know that the Lord alone was worthy of worship. And yet, God would redeem and save a remnant of Israel. The Lord will destroy every form of idolatry, but He will always save His people.

QUESTIONS

The Lord commanded Ezekiel to act out His messages. How do you think the impact might have been different if he had merely spoken them?

What does the visibility to the surrounding nations with which Israel and Judah were punished by God tell us about God's correction and discipline?

Chapter 6 calls out Israel for her idolatry. Reread the last sentence in the chapter. Why do you think this is significant?

Ezekiel 7-9

In Ezekiel 7, the Lord declares that the day for judgment has come. There was no more time for repentance.

"He is the answer to the longing in the hearts of the people He has made."

The people had every opportunity to repent and turn to Him, but they refused. The judgment for their sin would be great at the hands of the Babylonians. This judgment points us forward yet again to the judgment that will come at the end of days when Christ returns. There will be a time where there is no more opportunity to repent (Luke 14:15-23). While believers do not need to fear this time because we are secure in the righteousness of Christ, this should make us fearful for those who do not know Christ and have rebelled against Him. This finality is a serious matter, and we should think of it often as we interact with unbelievers. Judgment is coming, and there are lost souls who need to hear the good news that has changed our hearts and lives.

The people of Judah thought that their idolatry was hidden, but the Lord reveals to Ezekiel in chapter 7 that the leading elders are sacrificing to false gods in the Lord's temple. They either believed that the Lord did not care that they did so, or He did not see it happening, which is why they continued to do this in secret. This very attitude continues today when we actively live in hidden sin and think that the Lord does not see. Every action we take, thought we think, and word we say is on display before the Lord. When we are in Christ, our sin does not separate us from God because we are covered in His righteousness, but it can harm the depth and vitality of our relationship with Him. Hidden sin makes the life of believers miserable because they are being choked by the desires of the world (Mark 4:7).

The people of Judah did not realize that God knew exactly what was going on in His city, and He even was preparing to slay those who actively practiced idolatry and tried to hide it. He would protect those who did not commit this atrocity, but those who participated in it would face death—from the oldest in the city to the youngest. Ezekiel 9 can seem like a harsh chapter of Scripture as God's judgment is described, but the reality is that the consequence of sin

is death. Every breath we breathe on earth is a gift of mercy from the Lord because none of us deserve it. We must be careful to keep our own focus on the Lord. He is the only one worthy of our worship. His creation is nothing compared to the glory of our Creator. He is the answer to the longing in the hearts of the people He has made.

QUESTIONS

Reread Ezekiel 7:4. How does this verse deepen your understanding of God's disapproval and hatred of sin?

Spend some time in self-examination in light of the fact that Israel turned its back on the Lord while worshiping something created. In what ways are we prone to do something similar to God?

In chapter 9, we see that there are people who are marked and those who are unmarked. What is the significance of this? Why is this important to note?

Ezekiel 10-12

In Ezekiel 10, we find one of the most heartbreaking scenes of the entire book.

The glory of the Lord leaves the temple because of the people's rampant idolatry and continual rejection of God. Ezekiel gives us a depiction of the throne chariot of God coming to the temple and its courts and filling it, and then slowly moving from space to space. Finally, God's glory fully departs. This slow departure of God's glory reveals to us that He does not want to leave quickly. He gives more and more opportunity for His people to repent, but they do not. It is important to note that the glory of the Lord finally leaves through the eastern gate. When His glory returns at the end of Ezekiel, He will enter again through the eastern gate (Ezekiel 10:18-19). We will later see Jesus enter through the eastern gate when He rides on a donkey into Jerusalem the week before His crucifixion. It is here that He reminds His disciples that He is the King who has come for the people of God (Matthew 21:1-11). The glory of the Lord in flesh will soon come to Jerusalem. Though the Lord's presence left His city, and His judgment would be poured out for their sin, He would not leave forever. He would always desire to dwell with His people. Jesus's arrival gives evidence to that.

When Babylon collected their first group of exiles to leave Jerusalem, the king was taken, and a puppet king was left in his stead. Many of the wise leaders of Judah were also brought to Babylon, and evil, wicked men were left to give advice and counsel to the people. Ezekiel is instructed to prophesy against these leaders, and as he does so, one of them dies. Ezekiel is overwhelmed and wonders if the Lord is going to bring an end to the entire remnant of Israel. But God encourages Ezekiel that He will take care of the remnant of Israel's people. The Lord's presence had left the temple, but for the remnant of the Lord, He would be their sanctuary (Ezekiel 11:16). In these chapters—heavy with judgment—comes promises that will extend beyond Israel's present or even post-exilic period and far into the future for God's chosen people. The promise is that some would be cleansed of their sin and given a new heart and that some of the remnant of Israel would eventually return to their land.

"We can rejoice because we have been given new hearts to praise our Savior."

However, the new heart, new spirit, and spiritual regeneration described in Ezekiel 11:19-21 would not have an immediate fulfillment. The old covenant was good, but the new covenant Christ would bring would be better. The law had governed their actions, but the new covenant would transform their hearts (2 Corinthians 3, Hebrews 9-10). The new covenant is a promise that God will forgive our sins and restore us to Himself through the power of Christ's death and resurrection. As those who partake in the new covenant, we can rejoice that we can look back to the cross and see how our God has made redemption possible. We can rejoice because we have been given new hearts to praise our Savior.

QUESTIONS

What is the significance of the Lord's glory leaving the temple?

In what ways can we see hope in chapter 11?

Spend some time in prayer in light of Ezekiel 12:2, asking that God would open your eyes to see and your ears to hear His instruction and give you the strength to resist rebelling against Him.

Ezekiel 13-15

The book of Ezekiel is mainly about the false prophets of Judah.

These false prophets spoke as if they had a word from the Lord, but they did not. The false prophets ignored the problem of the heart and said what sounded good to the people. They preached peace when there was disaster soon to come. Like painting a rotting building witewhite wash, they tried to make the people feel better about their sin, but it could not cure their rottenness. The people needed to be pushed to holiness, not given a pep talk. The righteous remnants of God's people were able to see through these prophets' wickedness, but the unrighteous easily went along with what they said. Just as Israel was divided in Ezekiel 13, the message of the gospel is one of peace, but it is also divisive. Jesus's words reveal our broken condition and need for His righteousness, and yet there are many pastors and teachers who do not preach the divisive parts of what Christ says (Luke 12:49-53). Their avoidance is costly. The sin of man is great, and their need for the gospel is even greater. It is hard to hear how we are destined for sin without salvation from Christ, but the truth must be preached!

"Abiding in Jesus means that we remain in Him and remember our union with Him."

God reminds the people in Ezekiel 14 that He is bringing judgment because their hearts are full of idols. The Lord desired His people's hearts, and He knew that unless they faced judgment and suffering, they would continue to hold onto idols. Idolatry has been a repeated offense against God since the first sin of Adam and Eve. Every human born after them has dealt with idolatry and been guilty of it as well. God continues to use suffering as a means of removing idols from the lives of His people. While suffering is not always a result of holding onto idols, it can reveal any idols we cling to instead of the Lord. The Lord desires all of our hearts. He is not satisfied with His people being divided in their worship.

Ezekiel 15 again shows Israel as a useless vine because of her actions. Jesus will be the true Vine and the truer and better Israel. We will also be useless vines if we do not abide in Him. Apart from Him, we can do nothing, so we must stay close to the Vine. We must abide in Him and allow Him to work

in us. Abiding in Jesus means that we remain in Him and remember our union with Him (John 15). It is not another thing we have to do—it is a remembrance and gladness over our position in Christ. As we recognize our helplessness and are unified with Christ, we are given all spiritual blessing and no longer need to look to idols to save us. Instead of looking to idols, we will only continue to love Jesus more and more.

QUESTIONS

How can we identify false prophets? Read 1 John 4:1 to help answer.

Reread Ezekiel 14:3. What does it look like to "set up idols" in your heart? In what ways are you prone to this behavior?

Paraphrase chapter 15 in your own words.

Ezekiel 16–18

Ezekiel's vivid descriptions help us to clearly see how God's people were rejecting Him.

"He is ready to receive all who will return to Him."

The Lord describes Israel as a baby cast out into a field and left to die. Israel was abandoned and unwanted, but the Lord chose to make her His own. He adorned her with beauty and entered into a covenant with her. He became her faithful husband. But Israel, His bride, was prideful in her beauty and status, and she committed adultery with foreign nations. She rejected the One who had saved her and loved her. Israel would face discipline from her bridegroom for her wandering, but the Lord would remember His covenant with her. He would never abandon her and leave her to die. Instead, the Lord would deliver His bride from the shame of her sin. Ezekiel 16 is a picture of the gospel. We were the same as Israel, helpless and headed for death, but God redeemed us by the blood of Christ and brought us into His covenant family. May we never forget the Lord's faithfulness or put our trust in idols and worthless things that will never save us or love us as He will.

In Ezekiel 17, the Lord gives Ezekiel a riddle to speak to the house of Israel about two eagles and a vine. The riddle's purpose is to show the people the futility of trusting in anyone or anything other than the Lord. The first eagle represents King Nebuchadnezzar of Babylon. The top shoot of the cedar is King Jehoiachin. The vine is Prince Zedekiah, the puppet king who is set up to rule the land of Judah by Nebuchadnezzar when King Jehoiachin is taken to Babylon. The second eagle is Pharaoh. Zedekiah was an unfaithful vine, and he put his trust in Pharaoh rather than the Lord's plans for Judah under the rule of Nebuchadnezzar. Zedekiah's decisions would ultimately lead to his death and the deaths of his entire family. Unlike Zedekiah, Christ will be a faithful vine who will be faithful to the will of His Father. His faithfulness to the will of the Lord will lead to salvation for all who believe in Him. Jesus will fulfill the Lord's promise of a small twig that will be planted on top of a mountain and become a tree that every bird can dwell in. We will rest in the Righteous Branch and find our dwelling place in Him.

Ezekiel 18 shows us another picture of the mercy of God and a foreshadowing of the gospel. While God would not hold the people accountable for a sin

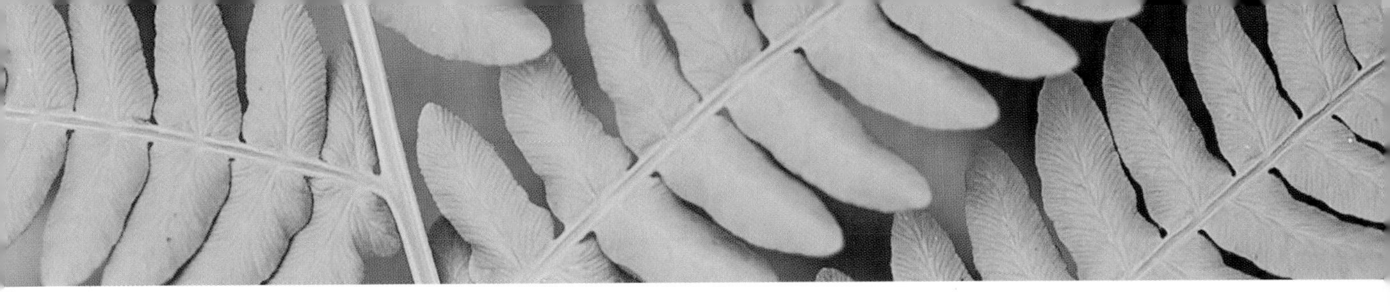

they did not commit, He would demand an answer for the sin of which they were guilty. And in the midst of terrifying prophecies of coming judgment, God tells His people to repent and live! If His people came back to them and admitted how they had wronged Him and looked to Him for redemption, He would provide it! But they would not come back. However, the Lord also offers us this mercy through Christ. We are given new hearts, and we are able to repent of our sins and live. He is ready to receive all who will return to Him.

QUESTIONS

What does chapter 16 show us about the deep love of God?

How does chapter 16 teach us about the depth of our sin and our inclination to wander from God?

Reread Ezekiel 18:30-32. How does this passage show us God's mercy, love, and justice?

Ezekiel 19–21

Ezekiel 19 contains a collection of two laments that would have been sorrowfully chanted aloud.

"Jesus is the true and better King promised to Israel."

The laments show the Lord's grief over the failure of Israel's leadership. The kings of Israel had failed miserably and fallen into sin. The people of Israel had always put their hope in God's promise to continue David's line, but they used this promise to excuse their sin. They thought that because God told David He would establish His throne forever, they would not face serious consequences for disobeying Him. But the people were wrong. The Lord suspended the line of David, and He brought judgment on the people (Ezekiel 19:12). Zedekiah will be the last king over God's people until Christ arrives. Jesus will carry on and establish the line of David forever. He will not be like the last three kings of Judah. He would be completely righteous and trustworthy.

Some of the elders of Israel, who were also in exile with Ezekiel, came to him to inquire of the Lord (Ezekiel 20:1). The Lord tells Ezekiel to demonstrate to them their hard-heartedness and rebellion by repeating scenes from Old Testament history. The pattern was always the same: the people rebelled, went after idols, and profaned the Lord's Sabbath. And while the people repeatedly did this, the Lord's response continued to be the same as well: He would restore and redeem His people for the glory of His name (Ezekiel 20:44). When the elders came to Ezekiel, they were still blind to their sin and how it was the same sin as their ancestors before them. The Lord will not hear from them. If left to our own devices, we would do exactly what Israel did, and we did follow the same pattern that they did before the intervention of the Lord on our behalf. Our salvation is not our own doing but the Lord's doing through Christ. He spares us from continuing to blindly repeat our mistakes, and He leads us in righteousness.

In Ezekiel 21, the Lord instructs Ezekiel to tell Jerusalem that His sword is drawn and about to strike. Ezekiel was to groan and display a broken heart and bitter grief. He would cry out and wail because of the Lord's coming judgment through Nebuchadnezzar. The Lord would lead the Babylonian king to His own city, and the Davidic line, which refers to King David's lineage, would seem lost once Nebuchadnezzar finished his conquest, but one

day an unexpected king would come. Jesus is the true and better King promised to Israel. He will hold all judgment in His hands, and He will draw His Sword, the Sword of the Spirit, the Word of God, to lead His people into truth (Ezekiel 21:27, Ephesians 6:17).

QUESTIONS

Ezekiel 20:8 cites Israel's unwillingness to listen to God as a partner in their rebellion against Him. Spend some time in prayer, asking God to soften you and make you more willing to listen to His instruction.

Reread Ezekiel 20:14. Why did God act for the sake of His name? What does this tell you about God's glory and holiness?

What does chapter 21 show you about the purpose for God expressing His justice in wrath?

Ezekiel 22-24

These chapters show the terrible depths of the sin of Israel. After all that the Lord had done for them, they continued to turn away from Him.

The nation was marked by injustice, idolatry, greed, lust, and even killing their children as sacrifices to idols. God's people had bent their morality and conscience to the evil world around them. Matters were only made worse by false prophets who made the people feel fine about their sin and claimed to have heard from the Lord when they had not (Ezekiel 22:25-26). The Lord would show Judah and the world His wrath toward sin, even if it meant destroying His chosen city. In Ezekiel 21, we are given an idea of the absolute wrath of God. This reminds us that Jesus did not just feel the pain of the crucifixion; He felt the pain of God's wrath, the wrath described as the fire of His fury (Isaiah 66:15). Jesus will live the life the people of Israel never could, and He will be our perfect substitute.

In Ezekiel 23, God compares Jerusalem and Samaria to two sisters who have committed grievous sexual offenses by being promiscuous and unfaithful to their husbands. He shows them how they have perverted the covenant relationship between Himself and them. The miserable ruin the sisters find themselves in because of their sin was the same end Jerusalem would meet if they continued to reject God and follow their own desires. We are just like these sisters who go after idols, and Jesus is our faithful bridegroom who rescues us and makes us His own.

Ezekiel 24 is a major turning point in the book as Ezekiel notes that Nebuchadnezzar has finally laid siege to Jerusalem. The Lord gives Ezekiel a vision that reveals the sinful attitude of the people as the siege begins. Israel believes that they are the choice meat in the pot of Ezekiel's vision, but the Lord will pour them into the fire, and they will be consumed at the hand of Nebuchadnezzar. Again we are reminded of the punishment Christ bore on the cross and that though we may think we are "good," our righteous works are like filthy rags. Only the righteous work of Christ is sufficient to satisfy God's wrath. We are continually and forever covered in it.

"We must stand for truth and cling to the unchanging One."

Our God is a God of justice, and He would not let His people's wickedness go unpunished. These chapters remind us that our own culture is not the first to bend its morality to the age in which we live. As believers, we must stand firm for the truth in a world that rejects it. We must be vigilant for justice and reject idolatry. In a world that changes and sways based on feelings, we must stand for truth and cling to the unchanging One.

QUESTIONS

Reread Ezekiel 22:17-22. What does this imagery mean? Read 1 Peter 1:7 for help.

How does the promiscuity spoken about in chapter 23 relate to idolatry?

What is the significance of the death of Ezekiel's wife?
What does this communicate to Israel?

Ezekiel 25-27

In the following three chapters, we not only see God's judgment for His people but His judgment for all of the nations, especially those who have delighted in the destruction of His holy city, Jerusalem.

It reminds us that for some of these nations, their destruction would be their end, but for others, it would be the avenue used by God to reveal the truth to those far from Him. Of the four nations God mentions in this chapter, three of them will know that He is the Lord by the judgment He brings. Edom is the only nation that will not. Even in His judgment, God desires for the world to turn to Him. Edom's fate represents the fate of those who are forever hardened in their sin and never turn to the Lord. We should be encouraged that though many will never accept the truth of the gospel, Jesus will draw men and women from every nation, even nations who seem as if they have abandoned God completely.

Even the nations God proclaims judgment on had access to His truth, but instead of turning to the Lord, they scoffed at God's people and built nations on their strength alone. Some, like Tyre, were great and mighty nations with prosperous economies. Tyre was one of the wealthiest trading cities in the world at that time. All the glory and beauty of the world could be found there, and all of the nations looked to Tyre in admiration to fulfill their desires (Ezekiel 27:3). The people of Tyre did not think that anything or anyone could ever bring them down. They set themselves up as being great, and yet the Lord would use Nebuchadnezzar to humble them. The people in Tyre are often associated with those who reject God. Their end is a pit of destruction in the world below (Ezekiel 26:20). We were once among these people, headed to the same pit, but God intervened on our behalf and transferred us from the kingdom of death and darkness to a kingdom of life. In Christ, we inherit "the land of the living" (Ezekiel 26:20).

And despite the people of Tyre's rejection of Him, the Lord asks Ezekiel to lament for them, showing His own heart for those who reject Him and are separated from Him forever. He does not desire that anyone should perish but that all men would come to know Him (2 Peter 3:9). May we possess the

"In Christ, we inherit 'the land of the living'"

same heart for our enemies and those who reject us because of the gospel— that they would come to a saving faith in Christ and experience the freedom from darkness and the pure joy from the beauty of the gospel.

QUESTIONS

How does chapter 25 communicate God's sovereignty to us?

What does the destruction of Tyre tell us about the character of God?

Chapter 27 tells us about the success of Tyre (by worldly standards). In what ways does this show us that earthly success is not necessarily indicative that the Lord is pleased?

Ezekiel 28-30

From the leaders of Tyre to the Pharaoh of Egypt to even Satan, these chapters focus on the sin of pride and those who are forever lost to its grip on their hearts.

"When we remember who we are and all God has done for us, we can live in humility and gratitude."

Though the city of Tyre was a real place with a real king, the Lord's description of the prince of Tyre ultimately describes the prince of this world, Satan himself. The thing that they had in common was that they viewed themselves much higher than they should have. They were filled with pride, and for each leader mentioned, their pride would bring about their destruction. They both set themselves up as gods even though they were not and never could be. And yet, even God raises a lament for them—even Satan. He was at one time blameless and full of beauty, but He rebelled against God and led humanity down the same path he took. Unlike the first human beings, Jesus will crush Satan forever and destroy the curse of sin (Genesis 3:15). And, unlike Satan and the other princes of this world, Jesus lives in perfect righteousness. He is the true King who will reign forever. Satan is an imposter who hides behind worldly wealth and beauty, and he will meet his end (Revelation 20:7-10).

The following four chapters contain judgment against Egypt. Egypt was one of the many nations that exemplified destructive pride. They attributed what came from the hand of God as coming from themselves and their gods. Even Pharaoh claimed to have made the Nile himself. All of these nations, however, were under the power of Almighty God. After Babylon would destroy Egypt, they would never control nations of the world in the same way again (Ezekiel 29:15, 19). Egypt was an old enemy of Israel. Egypt was the nation that enslaved them and from whom God had delivered them, as documented in Exodus. Yet Israel repeatedly returned to Egypt. The Lord would demonstrate once more to His people and Egypt that false gods could do nothing for them (Ezekiel 30:13).

Though we have already heard of God's victory through Christ on the cross, we often forget the beauty of the gospel and trust in ourselves and the idols of the world. God shows us these idols can do nothing for us and that Christ will ultimately destroy each and every one. We must be careful not to allow prideful attitudes that lead to idolizing ourselves and the world (Romans 12:3). Pride can sneak into our lives very subtly, and we must always be on guard against it. When we remember who we are and all God has done for us, we can live in humility and gratitude.

QUESTIONS

What does it look like to have a proud heart?
Why is this important to recognize?

What are some of the examples of pride that you see in chapters 28-30?
List them below.

What does Ezekiel 30:26 tell us about part of the purpose for discipline and judgment?

Ezekiel 31-33

In Ezekiel 31, we learn that the Pharaoh of Egypt will meet his end.

It is no coincidence that Pharaoh's crown had a serpent on top of it, representing Satan, the adversary of God. Just like the King of Tyre, Pharaoh will face destruction. We should not be surprised to know that Satan influences every evil and oppressive ruler. The downfall of these earthly rulers who believe that they are equal with God ultimately points to Satan's final destiny. The Lord gives a horrific description of the corpse of Pharaoh in Ezekiel 32. His corpse represents all of Egypt and those who reject God—they will be utterly ravaged and destroyed. The depiction of Pharaoh's destroyed corpse is a contrast to an approaching passage in Ezekiel that depicts the regeneration God offers to those who follow Him. Bones are resurrected and given flesh and new hearts. The bones of those who rebel against God will never experience this. Jesus will be victorious over the princes of the world. He is the true King who brings His people into peace with God rather than ruin.

Chapter 33 begins the last section of the book of Ezekiel, which will remind us of the hope of Israel. We see Ezekiel pictured as a watchman for Israel. The people would have been familiar with this role of one who stood on the city wall to warn of danger. Ezekiel was that for Israel, and now we are watchmen in our day, seeking to warn the world and point them to hope in Jesus. In Ezekiel 33, the Lord gives people another opportunity to return to Him and repent. But in verse 21, Ezekiel records a fugitive's arrival who tells Ezekiel that Jerusalem has fallen. God has done what He said He would do, and His judgment would be thorough. This arrival and completion of judgment will be the same at the end of the days, and we are like Ezekiel. We await the day and know it is coming, but we do not know exactly when Christ will return. However, we do know that this judgment will be even more terrifying than the judgment given to Jerusalem, as it will include the defeat of evil and death forever at the hand of Jesus.

The Lord's final call to repentance in Ezekiel 33 is a sobering reminder that one day it will be too late for repentance, and judgment will be set. This truth should urge us to share the gospel, knowing that the Lord will reveal the truth to those He has called.

"He is the true King who brings His people into peace with God rather than ruin."

QUESTIONS

In chapter 31, we see God harkening back to the imagery of the Garden of Eden. Why do you think this might be significant?

Reread Ezekiel 32:2. Compare and contrast what Pharaoh thinks of himself versus what the Lord declares him to be.

What is the role of Ezekiel as watchman? In what ways should we be watchmen in our present age?

Ezekiel 34-36

The judgments at the beginning of Ezekiel are giving way to promise after promise and reminders of our faithful God, who will never neglect His children.

The "shepherds" or leaders of Israel had let the people down and led them astray. Their selfishness had allowed for the spiritual decay of the city and its ultimate destruction. Now, God would rescue His people and be their shepherd. Ezekiel 34:23-24 contains a promise referring to Jesus, who will be the Good Shepherd God sets over His people. He will be a King from the line of David, and He will feed His sheep. We have been given eternal peace in Christ, but these verses also show us the peace and life of blessing we will have in eternity. Our future in Christ is full of beauty and hope (Ezekiel 34:25-31).

In Ezekiel 35 to 36, the Lord compares the mountains of Edom to the mountains of Israel. These mountains also represent those who reject the Lord and those who love Him. Edom had rejoiced and even contributed to the fall of Jerusalem, and God would destroy them. As Jerusalem was desolate after the Babylonian destruction, so Edom will also be. But the mountains of Jerusalem had a much different fate than the current situation they faced. They would be restored to their former glory, and the Lord would bring life, health, and beauty back to the land and His people. He would forgive their sins and dwell with them forever. The Lord did not do this because of any righteous works of the people but because He is merciful. The Lord does not only forgive our sins—He puts His Spirit in His people. He will become even more a part of them, and He will be closer to them than within the walls of the temple.

God will someday regather His chosen people, and Jesus will lead them. Chapter 36 tells of the changes that will happen in the hearts of the people, and these are things that have happened in us if we decide to follow Christ. He gives us new hearts, He has done this for us, and He will do it for Israel's remnant. He changes people from the inside out by giving them His Spirit. Once we have encountered Him, we will never be the same. Our God changes everything.

"Our God changes everything."

QUESTIONS

How does Psalm 23 help you to understand the imagery in Ezekiel 34?

Meditate on Ezekiel 34:11-16 tell us about God's character?
Does this passage remind you of any other passages in the Bible?

In what way does chapter 36 offer hope for Israel?

Ezekiel 37-40

Our God brings dead things to life (Romans 4:17). All of Scripture points to this glorious truth.

God brought Ezekiel to the Valley of Dry Bones to show the prophet what is possible in God's strength alone. Before Ezekiel lay an entire valley full of bones that by man's standard were hopeless and useless. But as Ezekiel spoke God's active Word to them and prophesied the breath of God over them, the impossible became a reality as the dry bones came to life (Ezekiel 37:10, Hebrews 4:12). Our God brings dead things to life. He can form great armies from dry bones, and He can transform the hearts of men from stone into flesh. This is the power of His Word. He can turn the hearts of His people back to Himself.

After the bones come to life, the scene shifts to the future, and we are given a picture of our beautiful inheritance through the gospel. Jesus is the perfect King who God promises at the end of this chapter, and He will be our King forever (Ezekiel 37:24-25). The Lord will give His people an everlasting covenant of peace, and He will dwell with us forever (Ezekiel 37:26-27). God will be faithful to His people. He will be faithful to Israel, and the promises in the New Testament say that He will be faithful to His church. This is the hope we have in Christ.

The next two chapters of Ezekiel are hard for commentators to decipher. The land of Gog has never been mentioned before in Scripture. Many commentators believe that Gog may be another name for Babylon, the city God will use to carry out His judgment. However, it is important to remember that Babylon also represents all of humanity who has rejected Him. We know for sure that God's people faced conflict and danger as the Lord brings them back to restore them, but the Lord promises that He will be their defense. Ezekiel's vision in these chapters also points to how the people of God will face trial yet again, even at the end of all things. But, God will consume the enemies of His people (Revelation 20:9). No enemy rivals the power of the Lord, and we can be confident in our great Savior who has conquered evil and death. Ezekiel 39 closes with yet another promise from the Lord to restore His people (Ezekiel 39:27-28). Evil will not thwart the promises of God.

"Evil will not thwart the promises of God."

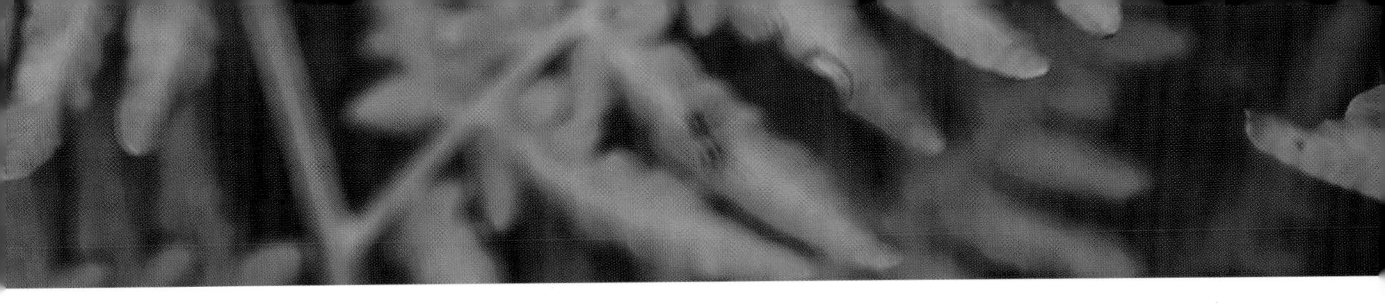

In Ezekiel 40, we begin to see the beginning of a series of chapters that will conclude this prophetic book. Fourteen years after the destruction of Jerusalem, the Lord gives Ezekiel a detailed tour of the future temple and Promised Land of His people. While the details in these chapters can be overwhelming, these chapters would have been immensely comforting to those in exile who had seen their temple and land go up in flames. They provided a seal of trust for the people to show God's promise was true, and He planned every part of their restoration! This should fill our hearts with joy to know that the promises of the new temple in Ezekiel are promises that we will one day see come to completion in eternity, as God will dwell in the midst of His people forever.

QUESTIONS

What symbolism do you see in Ezekiel 37:1-14?

Read Hebrews 4:12. How does this passage grow your understanding of the power of Scripture? In what ways is this verse on display in chapter 37 of Ezekiel?

What would the images described in Ezekiel 40 have meant to the exiled people in Babylon?

Ezekiel 41-44

The end of the book of Ezekiel looks to the future and the restoration of God's people.

These chapters detail Ezekiel's vision of the new temple. There are many opinions among scholars about whether this temple is a literal or figurative temple. The detail of the descriptions can lead one to believe that it is a literal temple. However, it is difficult to know for sure. Regardless of your opinion, these chapters point to God's majestic holiness and the necessity for us to worship Him.

In Ezekiel 41, the prophet continues to provide details about the temple and focuses on the inner places. It is important to note that Ezekiel includes descriptions of carved images of cherubim and palm trees as being on the temple's walls (Ezekiel 41:18). This should point us back to the beginning of the story of redemption, where God first dwelled with His people in Eden. The temple has always been a picture of that first dwelling place, and it also represents the future world that the people of God will inhabit. Cherubim, a type of angel, will be there, and this world will be full of trees and vegetation, and God will be with His people. Creation will finally reach its consummation (Revelation 21:22-22:3).

At the beginning of the book of Ezekiel, God's presence sadly left the temple, but in Ezekiel 43, His presence gloriously returns. What is even more wonderful is that He shuts the gate by which He first left, signaling that His presence will never leave the temple again. How Ezekiel describes the Lord's coming is how John later describes the sound of Christ's voice in Revelation (Ezekiel 43:2, Revelation 1:15). Though the people had sinned against God, God made a way for them to return to Him, and He chooses to dwell with them forever. Jesus's second coming in Revelation will signal our being brought into the presence of God forever. He will never leave us in heaven; we will always be with Him.

The end of chapter 44 reminds us that God is the inheritance of His people. As the people of God, we, like His people in Israel, are heirs of God (Ephesians 1:11-14, 18, 1 Peter 1:3-12). In this world, we will face opposition, but our inheritance in Him is more than we could have ever hoped for. There is something so much better to come for the people of God.

"There is something so much better to come for the people of God."

QUESTIONS

Do you see any symbolism in the construction of the new temple? Why might these things be significant?

What is the importance of the return of God's glory in chapter 43?

Summarize Ezekiel 44:28-31 in your own words.

Ezekiel 45-48

The book of Ezekiel is filled with declarations of judgment for sin and promises of ultimate redemption and restoration for the people who God loves.

Our God is a God of justice, and He will punish evil. But the judgment does not come without promises of mercy and calls to return to the Lord. The book ends with the extraordinary vision of a future temple in which God's people will worship Him for His holiness and faithfulness through all generations. In this future time, every promise that God has made to His people will be fulfilled. These promises have obliterated the hopelessness at the beginning of the book. The city of Jerusalem was destroyed, but God lets His faithful remnant see the new city they will dwell in forever. What a difference between the beginning of Ezekiel and the end of it!

In the last few chapters of Ezekiel, the prophet focuses on a figure called "the prince." We can assume that this prince is a reference to the coming Messiah, the fulfillment of the line of David, Jesus Christ. What is so interesting about the Prince's actions is that He is responsible for all of the offerings the people give to the Lord (Ezekiel 45:13-17). Jesus will one day absolve the sacrificial system because He is the perfect and final sacrifice given for the sins of God's people. And the inheritance of this prince will belong to His sons and servants (Ezekiel 46:16-18). Through Christ's atoning work on the cross, He has allowed us to become servants and children of the Most High God. Because of our union with Him, we inherit His inheritance. Our inheritance is the righteousness of Jesus and favor with God. We will never be separated from Christ, and our future is found in Him.

Just as the people of Israel who heard these prophecies only saw in part what was to come, we also only see in part. We wait for the day when we will see death and sin defeated and the completion of every promise at Christ's return. The Lord will keep every word of His promises, and we will be reminded of His sovereign hand and the treasure of redemption on the day when we are brought to our heavenly home to stay forever. For now, we wait in the tension of the "already and not yet," but someday, we will see every promise fulfilled.

"The Lord will keep every word of His promises."

QUESTIONS

What is the symbolism of the river described in chapter 47?

This section talks about land as the inheritance for different tribes. What is our inheritance in Christ? Read 1 Peter 1:18-21 for help.

Now that you have finished reading Ezekiel, what are some of the major themes of the book?

Yet we have not sought.

Daniel

GENRE: *Prophet, Exilic*

AUTHOR / DATE WRITTEN

Daniel • c. 605-530 BC

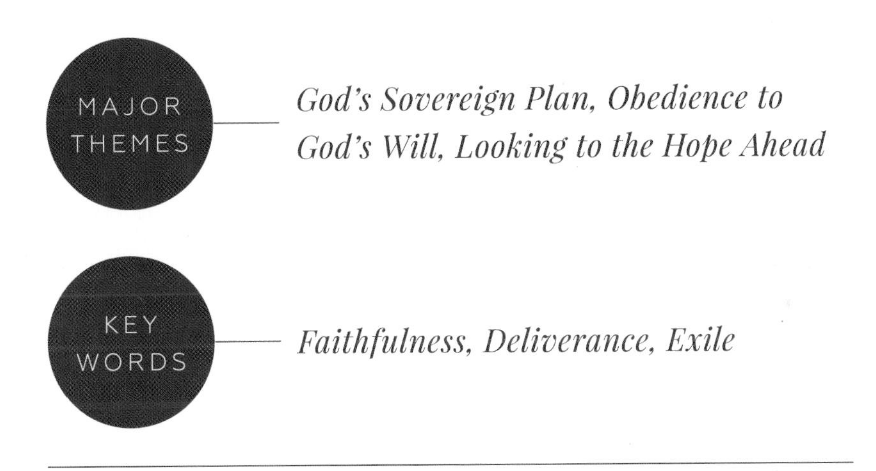

MAJOR THEMES — *God's Sovereign Plan, Obedience to God's Will, Looking to the Hope Ahead*

KEY WORDS — *Faithfulness, Deliverance, Exile*

KEY VERSE

DANIEL 9:13

Just as it is written in the law of Moses, all this disaster has come on us, yet we have not sought the favor of the Lord our God by turning from our iniquities and paying attention to your truth.

Daniel 1-3

The book of Daniel begins with several young men being carried off into captivity in Babylon.

Daniel is one of the first deportees from Jerusalem. He and others—who are either from royal families, nobility, or are attractive and wise young men—are brought into the king's court. Here, they will be taught the way of the Chaldeans, who were a group of people from southern Mesopotamia. In this foreign land, Daniel and his friends will demonstrate their faithfulness to the Lord, but more importantly, it is where God demonstrates His unfailing love and faithfulness to His people. God's goodness to Daniel and his friends beckons us to see that it is not because of our good works that the Lord is faithful to us and keeps His covenant; it is because of who He is and what Christ has done. God gave Daniel and his friends health, strength, and wisdom as they served in Nebuchadnezzar's court. They were an example to the Chaldeans of the blessing of walking with God and loving Him. Similarly, because of the gospel, we have access to all spiritual blessings in Christ and are called to demonstrate those blessings to a watching world.

"May our lives display to others the beauty of following Christ."

In Daniel 2, Nebuchadnezzar has a troubling dream and is losing sleep and peace of mind. He gives his wise men the impossible request of telling him the dream he had and then interpreting its meaning. If they cannot follow through with this task, they will be put to death. The wise men tell him that there is no one alive who could do as the king requests, but this only infuriates him more. Nebuchadnezzar orders all of the wise men in the land to be executed. When Daniel hears of this, he seeks the Lord, and the Lord faithfully reveals Nebuchadnezzar's vision to him. Even in the "wisest" of men, human wisdom is limited, but God's wisdom never ends. He is the source of wisdom. Daniel will give God credit for revealing Nebuchadnezzar's vision to him and its interpretation. The vision shows that there are kingdoms coming that will surpass Babylon, but they will all be nothing compared to the kingdom of God; the kingdom Jesus announces has come when He begins His ministry. Even though Jesus's kingdom is different from the kingdoms of the world, it is the most powerful kingdom there has ever been and ever will be.

Because of Daniel's interpretation, he is promoted as ruler over the city of Babylon, and Daniel promotes his friends as well. His friends, Shadrach, Meshach, and Abednego, are thrown into the spotlight when they refuse to worship an idol made by Nebuchadnezzar. Nebuchadnezzar realizes the God of Israel is powerful, but he still does not claim Him as the one true God. Nebuchadnezzar's decision to cast the three men into the fire for their refusal to worship his idol will only be another opportunity the Lord uses to display His power and authority over all false gods and idols. When the Lord saves Daniel's friends from the fire, Nebuchadnezzar worships God, but he still does not follow Him. Similarly, some see the power of the gospel, but they do not have a relationship with Christ. May our lives display to others the beauty of following Christ.

QUESTIONS

Read James 1:5 and then focus on Daniel 1:17-21. How do these passages reveal God to be the giver of wisdom?

What does Daniel's praise of God in Daniel 2:20-23 reveal about God's character?

Meditate on Daniel 2:44-45. How do these verses offer hope to us today?

Daniel 4-6

At the beginning of Daniel 4, we see that Nebuchadnezzar—the mightiest king in the world—is shouting the praises of God.

"Persecution of the saints brings an opportunity for others to hear the gospel."

Bringing the people of Judah into exile was not only for the people's judgment. It was also to show God's glory to the nations. And yet, Nebuchadnezzar asks David to interpret another one of his dreams because he "a spirit of the holy gods is in him" (Daniel 4:8). Daniel makes it very clear that the Lord is the One who works within him, but Nebuchadnezzar still does not see the truth. Nebuchadnezzar's dream depicts a large and beautiful tree that is strong and fruitful, but the tree will be cast away and destroyed. Daniel tells Nebuchadnezzar that he is the tree. Nebuchadnezzar will set himself up as higher than God in his own eyes, and the Lord will bring him low. It is finally in Nebuchadnezzar's humiliation that he calls upon the Lord, and the Lord restores him. Nebuchadnezzar repents, unlike many of the people of Judah, and God is faithful to him. God offers us restoration, and His kingdom is the true and better tree that will give its citizens strength, nourishment, and eternal security (Mark 4:30-32).

The narrative immediately moves on to the reign of Nebuchadnezzar's son, Belshazzar. Belshazzar is full of the passion and lust of the world. He has not followed his father in humbling himself before the Lord. In fact, during one of his feasts, he takes the holy vessels from the Lord's temple and instructs his lords, wives, and concubines to drink from them. Belshazzar's response to the Lord is a contrast to Nebuchadnezzar's repentance. He demonstrates life in rebellion and contempt of the Lord. However, the Lord will quickly judge Belshazzar and bring an end to his kingdom. The Lord has a hand appear on one of the walls at Belshazzar's wicked feast, and it ominously writes a message of judgment (Daniel 5:5-12). When Daniel reveals what the message means, Belshazzar does not repent; he only tries to cover up his wrongdoing by honoring David and giving him authority in his kingdom, a kingdom that Daniel knows is about to fall. Belshazzar is killed that very night. Nebuchadnezzar and Belshazzar's lives are reminders to us of the two responses we can have to the message of the gospel—either we repent and are given new life, or we rebel and continue in spiritual death.

The Babylonian kingdom will fall to the Medes and Persians, and Darius the Mede will be the next king Daniel will serve under. Daniel continues to succeed and is favored by this new king because of the wisdom God gave him. God consistently cares and provides for Daniel, even when he is thrown into a lion's den for his worship of the Lord, and deliverance seems impossible (Daniel 6). Our obedience to Jesus will glorify His name. Persecution of the saints brings an opportunity for others to hear the gospel. An example of this is when Daniel leaves the lion's den, Darius, a pagan king, praises God. Because of stories like Daniel's, we can trust that Jesus will deliver us from our enemies.

QUESTIONS

What does Daniel 4 teach you about the value of humility?

In what ways do we see God's faithfulness and gifting of Daniel in these passages?

How does Daniel's example in chapter 6 encourage you to strengthen your prayer life?

Daniel 7-9

There is a shift in the book of Daniel in chapter 7. The book moves from Daniel's life in Babylon to the recording of Daniel's dreams and prophecy for the future events of the end times.

It is easy to become overwhelmed by the details of these prophecies, but we must remember that we can remain confident that our God will ultimately be victorious. As Daniel's first vision begins, he sees four beasts representing the four nations from Nebuchadnezzar's visions earlier in the book. But these beasts and kingdoms are overshadowed as the Lord, "the Ancient of Days," takes a seat on His throne (Daniel 7:9). Then, Daniel sees a preincarnate appearance of Jesus. As a reminder, seeing preincarnate Jesus means that someone saw Jesus before He became man, as documented in the New Testament. In Daniel, the preincarnate Jesus looks like a "Son of Man" who comes before the Lord (Daniel 7:13). This is a beautiful reminder of how Jesus brings hope in the midst of chaos. We can rest assured that—in a world that is constantly changing—His kingdom will never pass away.

Daniel's visions continue in chapter 8. We should take note of how Daniel begins these visions by reminding us of when he had them. Many of them are during the reign of King Belshazzar. When Daniel approached Belshazzar to interpret the ominous writing on the wall, the fall of the Babylonian kingdom was no surprise to Daniel. The Lord showed him that this would be the fate of the empire. As the Lord continues to point Daniel toward the things of end times, Daniel is alarmed at what he sees. The ultimate message we can take from these visions is that God rules all, and Christ is victorious. Every event in the world around us has been ordained and purposed by the Lord.

Chapter 9 contains a shift in tone from visions to Daniel's prayer to the Lord as a plea for his people. Daniel has lived in Babylon for a long time, and he goes before the Lord in sackcloth to pray and weep for his people and to prepare for the end of the seventy-year captivity that he has read about in Jeremiah's prophecies. Daniel focuses on the faithfulness and mercy of God in his prayer. The people have been faithless to the Lord, but He has always been faithful to them. Daniel's prayer is beautiful and is a picture of our hope

"We have eternal peace and security through Christ."

in the gospel. We echo his words in verse 18. We do not rely on our righteousness as we plead and speak to the Lord; we rely on His great mercy. Gabriel, the man who explained the vision in chapter 8, comes to Daniel and gives him understanding. Gabriel also tenderly reminds him that Daniel is greatly loved. Gabriel explains what the restoration of Jerusalem will soon look like, but he also touches on its eventual destruction. Because of Christ's sacrifice, the temple will no longer be necessary, and the Lord's people will worship Him all across the world. We can rest in the knowledge that just like Daniel, we are tenderly loved by God, and because we are His children, we have eternal peace and security through Christ.

QUESTIONS

Why might it be important to recognize the shift in this section from narrative to prophecy?

Think about the name "Ancient of Days." What does this name reveal to us?

What does chapter 9 teach you about prayer?

Daniel 10–12

The final chapters of Daniel contain one vision.

As Daniel sees unseen things happening around him in the spiritual realm, we remember that there are unseen spiritual battles around us as well (Daniel 10:18-21, Ephesians 6:12). Once again, an angelic being who appears as a man clothed in linen comes to Daniel and repeatedly strengthens him and reminds him that he is greatly loved. The Lord loves when His people come to Him in humility, and Daniel exemplified a humble heart throughout his entire life. As Daniel listens to the man clothed in linen, he learns that there are spiritual beings who fight for the people of God. While hearing about unseen spiritual battles may cause us to be frightened, we have nothing to fear. We have been given a great Savior who fights for us.

Daniel gives one of the most detailed prophecies in the entire Bible in chapter 11. Many people claim that it was written later as history instead of prophecy because of how specific it is about events that would happen up to 375 years in the future. But we know that the Lord is all-wise and all-knowing, and He could have revealed anything He pleased to Daniel. Even before the fall, God knew each event in history and how He would carry out His story of redemption. His redemptive work involved the kingdoms of the world, and there would even be some who would leave their homelands to follow Him. This chapter also reveals that God's people will endure trials and hardship, but that we do not need to be disheartened because this world is not our forever home! Even though we do not know all of the details of what is to come, we know Christ is victorious (John 16:33).

Daniel was a man of purpose, prayer, humility, and conviction. The Lord gave him great insight into future events and what was ahead for God's people. Daniel got just a glimpse of the spiritual warfare at work in the world, but he was not paralyzed by it. Instead, he allowed it to push him further toward the Lord, prayer, and his purpose. He lived in a time when his faith was ridiculed, and yet he never let his faith in the Lord waiver. There must have been many times that he did not understand what was ahead, but he always turned to the Lord.

"We can live boldly like Daniel because we serve the same faithful God."

Many prophecies in this book are valuable to study, but we must remember that each one points us to a sovereign God who will keep His promises to His people. Even when we do not understand, we can trust Him. We can live boldly like Daniel because we serve the same faithful God.

QUESTIONS

Meditate on Daniel's vision in Daniel 10:5-9. Why do you think this vision impacted Daniel so profoundly?

What does chapter 12 tell us about the future?

Now that you have finished reading Daniel, spend some time in reflection. What are some of the most impactful things this book has taught you?

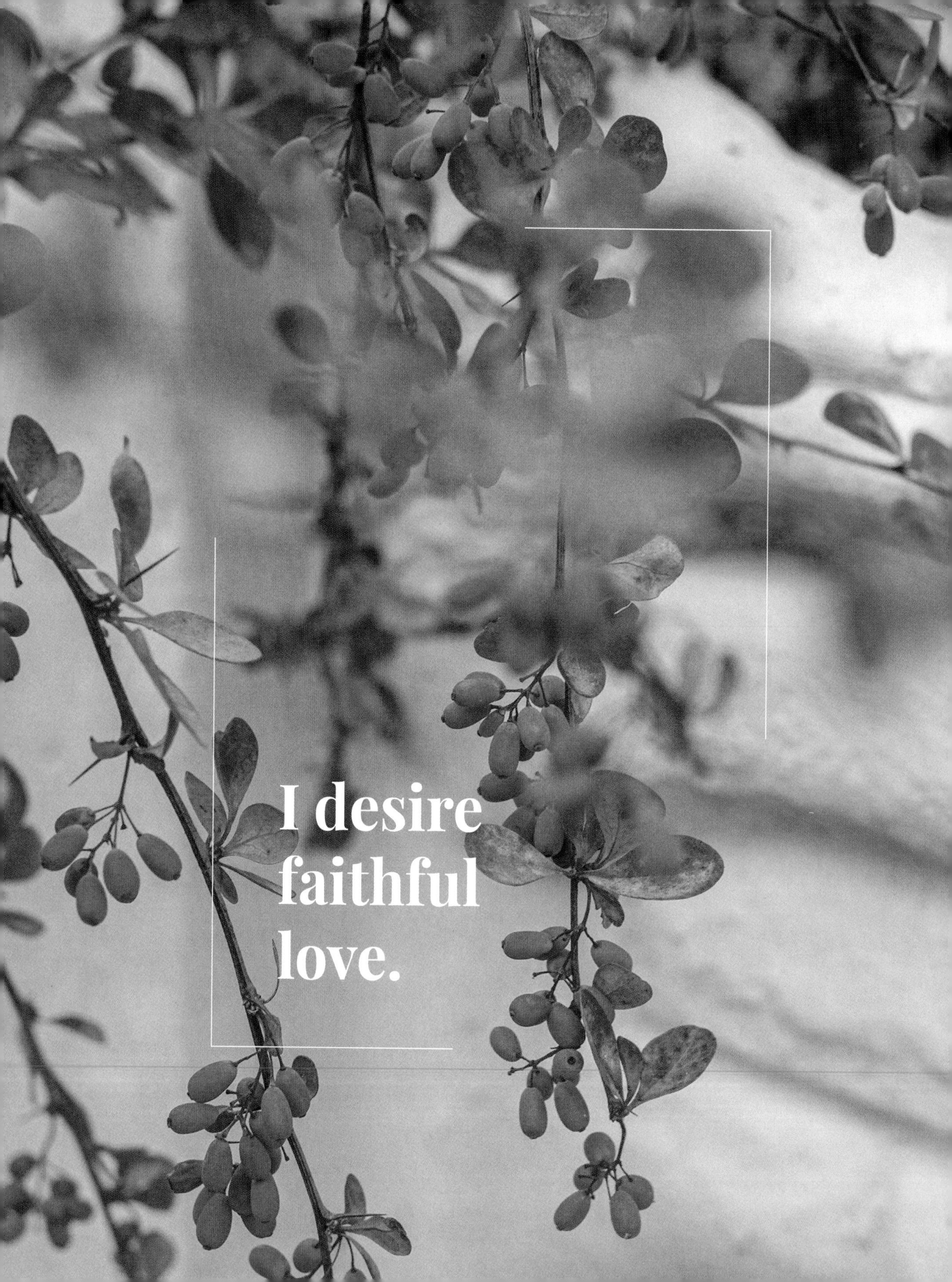
I desire
faithful
love.

Hosea

GENRE: *Prophet, Pre-exilic*

AUTHOR / DATE WRITTEN

Hosea • c. 755–725 BC

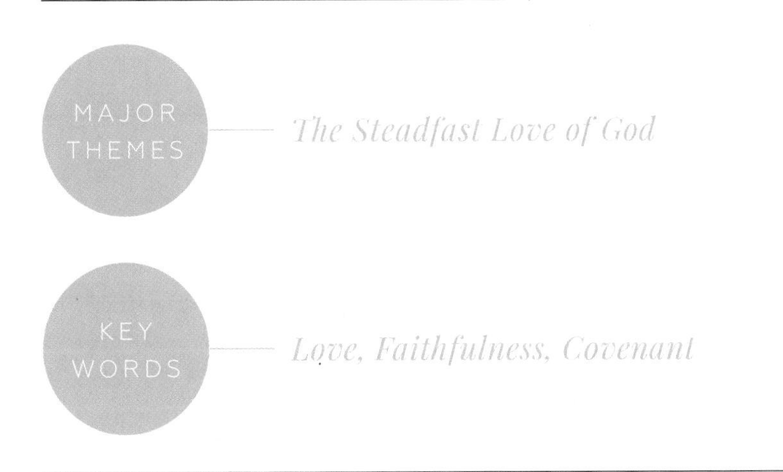

KEY VERSE

HOSEA 6:6

For I desire faithful love and not sacrifice, the knowledge of God rather than burnt offerings.

Hosea 1-3

The book of Hosea gives us a beautiful picture of the steadfast and unfailing love of our God.

"Jesus gives us direct access to the Lord and restoration with Him forever."

God called Hosea to live out a sermon by marrying a prostitute named Gomer, who would be unfaithful to him. Hosea's marriage to Gomer would be a symbolic representation of the Lord and the people of Israel. As Hosea and Gomer began to have children, the Lord instructed Hosea to give them symbolic names that displayed a reversal of the language God typically used to convey His promises and love for His people. God had chosen Israel and given Himself to them as a faithful husband, but they forsook Him and prostituted themselves to foreign gods. However, this reversal of the covenant language would not be their end. Immediately after the judgment of Israel, which is given through the names of Hosea's children, the Lord tells Hosea that Israel will one day again be known as His children, and He will gather them up from exile.

In chapter 2, God pleads with His people to turn from their sins, but they ignore His warnings. God brings Israel into exile so that they will see the foolishness of their idol worship and realize that He alone is their hope. His punishment of His people would ultimately bring their salvation. The Lord would again speak tender words to Israel and restore their covenant and relationship. This pattern can also be seen in the life of a believer. We have been saved by the glorious grace of the gospel, but we often put our trust in idols and things of the world. The Lord, our faithful Father, disciplines us and strips us of these idols so that our relationship with Him will continue to thrive. It is important to note that while our sin does not separate us from God after we have been justified in Christ, it does prohibit us from knowing God more intimately and experiencing true joy in Him. The hope of heaven is that we will finally be free of the presence of sin. Just as God, through His divine judgment, will completely remove Baal worship from the land, so through Christ's return to earth, will He destroy sin and death forever.

Our God restores even the most broken things, and He always seeks to bring the wanderer home. God would command Hosea to act out this very attribute of Himself by seeking out his unfaithful wife, buying her back from

adultery, and promising her restoration (Hosea 3). In the same way, God would return His people to the land from their exile and restore them. The restoration of all of God's people to Himself would not be consummated until the coming of Christ. Jesus gives us direct access to the Lord and restoration with Him forever.

QUESTIONS

Think about the names given to Hosea's children. In what ways are these significant, and what do they communicate to you about Israel?

In what ways is God's love expressed through Hosea's love for his wife?

Meditate on Hosea 3:1. In what ways are we unfaithful to God? How has God come to you time after time to show you His love and faithfulness?

Hosea 4-6

The people of Israel were far from the Lord. They followed their desires and the gods of other nations while neglecting the true God who pleaded for their hearts.

They felt self-sufficient, and the more they prospered, the more they thought they did not need the Lord. Because of this, there was a pervasive lack of knowledge of God. Instead of faithful worship and adoration of the true God, worship of false idols abounded. But sin never satisfies, and the people of Israel would have to answer for their rebellion against God. The Lord is the only thing that truly satisfies the longing in our souls. The rebellion of Israel reveals the rebellion of every man and woman who has ever been born. We run after man-made pleasure, and we forsake the true Creator, the God of the universe, who desires to be known by us. And yet the Lord waited in mercy and steadfast love for His people to return to Him, and He has mercy and steadfast love for us. We have seen it in the beauty of the gospel.

Because of the people's sin, they would face destruction and exile, but instead of returning to God and repenting, they would look for help from the nation that would be the very one the Lord would use to carry out their coming judgment (Hosea 5:13). The nations of the world could not heal them or save them. Only the Lord had the salvation they needed, but they did not know Him. When we look at the world around us, we can see the devastation of an absence of knowledge of God. It creates havoc and chaos, and it causes humanity to look to people and material possessions for salvation. These are all the false idols of our current age, and they are just as destructive as the Baals in the time of Canaan. Let us preach the gospel, the only hope for the world, to people who desperately need the healing of Jesus. May we demonstrate a love of the Lord, and let us learn from the failures of Israel and pass down this knowledge to the next generation so love and faithfulness to Christ will continue.

Chapter 6 begins with Hosea's urgent cry to the people to return to the Lord. The words of Hosea are beautiful and comforting. If the people returned to God, He would heal and revive them. He would raise them so they could be in a relationship with Him. Everything about the Lord was filled with safety, security, and peace, but the people's love for the Lord was not strong or last-

"The unchanging nature of God gives us hope in the gospel."

ing. It quickly faded, even amidst the precious promises of God. The people were just like their ancestor, Adam, who broke their covenant with God in the garden of Eden. We are just the same. We are unable to truly show the Lord lasting and enduring love. It is only because He gives us new hearts that we can love and obey Him. However, His love for us will never change. The unchanging nature of God gives us hope in the gospel.

QUESTIONS

What type of knowledge do you think Hosea 4:6 is talking about? Why is this significant?

Reread Hosea 5:15. How do we acknowledge our own guilty action and seek the Lord? What are some practical ways to do this?

Meditate on Hosea 6:1. In what ways do you see God's grace and discipline displayed in this verse?

Hosea 7-10

As people continued to reject the Lord, He was never changing and stood ready to redeem (Hosea 7:13).

However, Israel did not remember that the Lord knew and saw all of their evil. The people lived in their own strength and sin, even though the sovereign God was ready to help them and save them from their wickedness. This is a reminder to us of our need to call upon the Lord in our sin. Confession in the life of a believer is healthy and important (James 5:16). It is a tool the Lord uses to lead us away from sin. Calling out to God in our brokenness and exposing our sin will ensure that it will not have a stronghold in our lives. God offered this same healing to Israel, but instead of turning to Him, they looked for help from other nations. These nations would be the same ones that would destroy them (Hosea 9:6). Let us look to Jesus and the riches of God's grace for the help we need instead of the decaying and useless things of the world.

Hosea 8 contains more reasons for Israel's exile. As the people rejected God and lived in darkness, they hypocritically tried to claim that they knew Him, but their actions displayed the opposite. Instead of worshiping God, they set up idols and kings to replace Him. They patterned their lives after the surrounding nations and became just like them. Believers of Jesus face the same temptation. We accept the gospel with joy, and then we become used to the blessings and incredible gifts of hope that we have in Jesus. We are then comfortable and turn to worldly things instead of Jesus for satisfaction (1 John 2:15, James 1:14-15). We have access to the Creator of the universe, who is so much better than the hope the world offers.

"Jesus is the true and better Vine."

In chapter 9, Hosea shows the people the result of living in contrast to how the Lord calls them to live. Because they forsook the Lord and prostituted themselves to other gods and nations, they will not remain in the Lord's land, and they will face destruction. God will reject them as they have rejected Him. One of the most staggering things the Lord says to them is that He will no longer love them (Hosea 9:15). Israel had experienced the blessings of God, but then they turned and worshiped other idols that had nothing to do with what they received from the Lord. They were an unfaithful vine (Hosea 10:1). Jesus is the true and better Vine that allows those who know and love Him to bear fruit because they are in union with Him (John 15). God was calling Israel to be

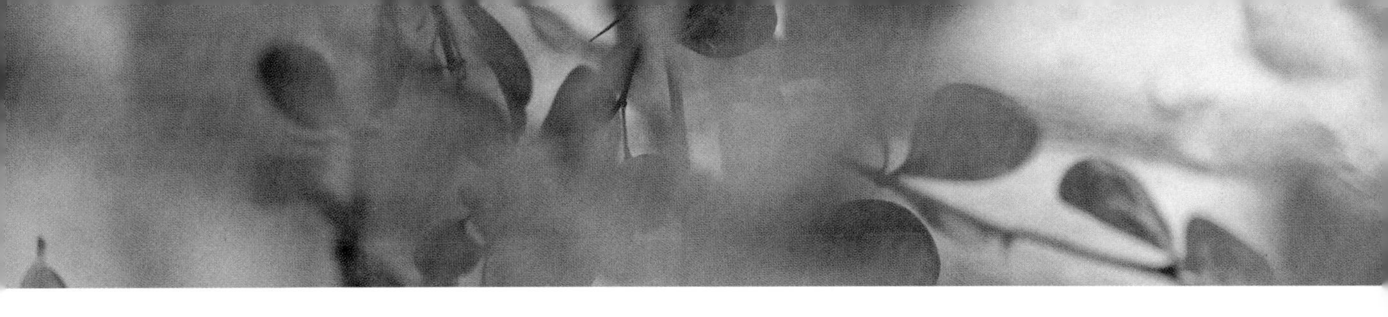

like Him and to follow His way instead of their way. He desired to return to them, to put His love on them, and to rain righteousness and goodness upon them. Because we are in Christ, the Lord gave us His righteousness even though we did not pursue Him in the first place (John 3:16). We are just like Israel, lost in our way and unwilling to repent, but God intervened and saved us through His Son.

QUESTIONS

Reread Hosea 7:13. How does this verse illustrate to you God's willingness to forgive us alongside His requirement that we repent from our sin and return to Him?

Think about the imagery used in Hosea 8:7. What are some ways that we are prone to "sow the wind"?

What are some ways that we can sow righteousness and reap steadfast love, as shown in Hosea 10:12?

Hosea 11-14

God had been faithful to His people, and in chapter 11, we see a tender love poem between them.

Despite their rejection and rebellion against Him, the Lord could not bear the thought of separation from Israel. He was full of compassion and love for them. And God's love and kindness should have led them to repentance (Romans 2:4), but instead, they continued to reject Him. God pleaded with them to return, and He offered His help. God had been with them from the beginning. He was their God, and He had carried them through the hardest days, but when life got easier, they forgot Him. People often look at the God of the Old Testament as only being angry, and though He is certainly full of righteous and holy wrath toward sin, it is because that sin destroys the people He loves. His love and wrath go hand in hand. He promises He would one day faithfully gather His people back to Himself.

In chapter 12, Hosea looks back at the redemptive history of the people of Israel and brings up example after example of how they have always committed the same sins against the Lord. They are sought out by God, blessed by Him, and share in His covenant, but then they decide to rebel and reject His ways. The Lord punishes them and seeks to restore them to Himself. The pattern repeats again and again. We are exactly the same, and we should not look down on the people of Israel for their repetitive sin, but it is right for us to learn the history of God's people so that we become aware of how we are prone to make the same mistakes.

In chapter 13, the Lord takes time to call the people to remember who He is and how He had always been with them and for them, unlike their man-made idols and kings. We need to remember this too! Pausing to consider how God has restored us and who He is helps us to be filled with gratitude and love for Him. It lets us rejoice over all the good He has done! May we not allow our successes to overshadow the giver of all good things. May we cling to Him in good times just as much as in trials.

The book closes with a beautiful reminder of who God is and what He does. He receives. He restores. He revives. God's people had drifted, and He pleaded in mercy for them to return. This is how our God loves us. Though we wander, He calls us back to Himself. His arms are open wide to call the wayward home (Luke 15:20).

"Though we wander, He calls us back to Himself."

QUESTIONS

Reflect on the imagery used in Hosea 11:3-4. What does this tell you about the character of God?

Reread the last verse of the book. In what ways does this encourage you and give you hope?

Now that you have finished reading the book of Hosea, what are some of the major precepts that God has taught you?

Turn
to me.

Joel

GENRE: *Prophet, Pre-exilic*

AUTHOR / DATE WRITTEN

Joel • c. 835-800 BC

Judgment of Covenant Disobedience, Restoration from the Lord

Day of the Lord, Repentance

KEY VERSE

JOEL 2:12

Even now—this is the Lord's declaration—turn to me with all your heart, with fasting, weeping, and mourning.

Joel 1-3

The book of Joel is very short compared to the other prophetic works, but it carries a meaningful message to God's people to prepare for the day of the Lord.

"God's grace, mercy, and kindness compel us to run to Him in repentance."

Joel ministered during the reign of Joash, and he used the current events of the day to speak the truth in a way that the people would understand. It is important to note that he does not directly accuse the audience of specific sins because he is expecting that the listeners and readers of his messages would already be familiar with the sins of the people. In chapter 1, Joel urges the people to tell their children about the Lord so that they could carry on the truth to each generation. Joel describes a plague of locusts that reminds us of the plague the Lord gave to Egypt (Exodus 10), but now this plague is being carried out against Israel. Joel calls Judah to repent because the coming locusts were a symbol of the day of the Lord. The term "day of the Lord" refers to God's judgment day.

The first fulfillment of this fateful day comes at the hand of a foreign nation that would invade Judah, but the ultimate fulfillment of the day of the Lord is yet to happen. As seen in the book of Revelation, the coming day of the Lord will be when Christ comes, accompanied by His heavenly army to set up His kingdom (Joel 2:2). Joel indicates through a rhetorical question that no one without Christ can endure the day of the Lord. Without the righteous work of Christ on the cross, we would also look at the day of the Lord with great hopelessness. But because we are united with Christ, this day should bring us great joy. This day will mark the church's physical reunion with Jesus, and there will be no separation from Him ever again. It also is the day when God will destroy evil and death, and we will be free from sin forever. The curse of Adam and Eve will be no more.

The Lord does not leave the people in hopelessness. He tells them to return to Him, and He reminds them of who He is (Joel 2:13). Our return and repentance are only possible because of the graciousness and mercy of God. God will always defend and sustain His people, and the greatest picture of this is in Jesus's death and resurrection on the cross, the Lord's ultimate provision for salvation. Joel even describes the day of Pentecost, the glorious day when the

Holy Spirit is poured out onto the people of God (Joel 2:28-32). The Spirit of God is given to us through the gospel, and God physically dwells inside His people. The final verses of Joel end with Jesus dwelling and reigning over Jerusalem. We will dwell in the house of the Lord because of Christ. Though our sin is as great as the people of Israel, God's grace, mercy, and kindness compel us to run to Him in repentance (Joel 2:12-13, Romans 2:4).

QUESTIONS

Reread Joel 1:1. How does this first verse give us reason to trust the integrity of what Joel is about to proclaim?

Summarize the book of Joel in your own words.

Now that you have read the book of Joel, what are some of the main, overarching themes?

Hate evil
and love
good.

Amos

GENRE: *Prophet, Pre-exilic*

AUTHOR / DATE WRITTEN

Amos • c. 767–743 BC

God Urging Repentance for Social and Moral Injustices, Judgment on the Rebellious, Future Hope and Restoration through the House of David

Injustice, Judgment

KEY VERSE

AMOS 5:15

*Hate evil and love good; establish justice in the city gate.
Perhaps the Lord, the God of Armies, will be gracious
to the remnant of Joseph.*

Amos 1-3

Amos is an example of how God can use anyone to accomplish His purposes. Amos was a humble shepherd, and yet God used him to be a great prophet.

In Amos 7:14-15, Amos pointed out that he was not a prophet or a prophet's son, but God chose him right where he was in a field herding sheep to prophesy to the nation. God can use anyone, and He looks for those who are willing to surrender to His call. The book of Amos begins with six judgment sermons on the nations surrounding Israel. These nations oppressed and brutalized each other. They disregarded the sacredness of God's image by thoughtlessly and cruelly destroying human life. However, the Lord had been patient with them. He did not destroy these nations after only a few mistakes and gave them opportunities to turn and repent. The gospel also reveals the Lord's patience with us. Through the gospel, the Lord has restored us to the lives we were meant to live, even though we are still in a world tainted with sin.

In chapter 2, the Lord's judgment turns toward His people, Judah and Israel. God reminded them of their past and how He had delivered them, but He also warned them that there would be judgment if they did not turn to the Lord. When the Lord speaks of the sins of His people, they did not sound like God's chosen people; they sounded like a foreign nation that did not know God. They set themselves up as higher than God, and they oppressed others for their own pleasure. They loved wealth and riches more than God. This reminds us that even God's church—those who are supposed to know God—act out in rebellion and disobey God's Word, for the church is made up of fallen human beings. Our sin does not separate us from the Lord because of our justification in Christ, but it does have to be addressed for us to grow (Romans 3-4).

God's people were so blinded by their sin that Amos said that they did not even know how to do right (Amos 3:10). Yet even in their sin, God sent them the prophet Amos to warn them and plead with them to repent and turn to Him. God used an ordinary man to proclaim His steadfast love for His people. Though the people's hearts and worship were far from God, He sought to bring them back to Himself and restore them.

"Through the gospel, the Lord has restored us to the lives we were meant to live..."

QUESTIONS

What does the fact that God used a shepherd to prophesy to His people teach us about His character? What does this tell us about qualifications and obedience?

How do these chapters provide a cautionary tale for us about the dangers of relying on our earthly prosperity?

Meditate on Amos 3:10. What does this show you about your own need and God's character?

Amos 4-6

Chapters 4 to 6 of Amos reveal the main reasons as to why the Lord is bringing judgment upon His people.

The people of Israel had the appearance of being religious and did all the right things, but their hearts were far from the Lord. Their sin separated them from God just as Isaiah had spoken of in Isaiah 59:1-2. God had pleaded with them to return, but they would not. The people found their security in their prosperity, wealth, and their extravagant lifestyles. The Lord describes a series of misfortunes He gave His people to remind them that He was God and encourage them to return, but they would not. These misfortunes are similar to the plagues that the Lord carried out against Egypt in Exodus. It should have caused the people to remember these events from their history (the Lord even references Egypt in Amos 4:10), but they did not. God repeats patterns in redemptive history for the sake of His people so that they will remember, repent, and return to Him.

God called for His people to seek Him and live. He pleaded for them to hate evil and love good. When we seek the Lord, we will be transformed to become more like Him. Our desires and actions will become like His, and we will escape spiritual death. The people of Israel did not seek or worship the Lord. They sought their own pleasure and comfort. They went through the tradition and ritual of worship for the Lord but then lived lives that were completely opposite of what He called them to. Without Christ, our hearts are just the same as theirs. It is only because of Jesus that we can hate evil, our natural human inclination, and love what is good. The gospel gives us life and access to God through the death and resurrection of Christ, and it helps us then live for the things of God. We begin to desire His justice and righteousness for the people around us, and we begin to hate injustice and oppression. The Lord was tired of His people's hypocrisy and fraudulent worship of Him. As we read these chapters, we should reflect carefully and think about how we may imitate Israel's behavior. How do we show outward worship but then have cold hearts toward God?

"May we be people that seek Him above all else."

The people of Israel thought they had plenty of ease and security in the promises of the Lord. They thought they could continue to sin, and He would overlook it. The Lord responds to this way of thinking by destroying

His own house, something Israel never thought He would do. He would raise nations against them. We are secure in Christ, but we should not take lightly the grace we have received. This life can encourage us to rest in earthly ease and security, but our hope and rest must be in Jesus. There were so many things that were distracting the people of Israel from the Lord, and the same can be true for us if we allow it to be the case. May we be people that seek Him above all else.

QUESTIONS

Notice the repetition of the phrase, "yet you did not return to me" in chapter 4. What does this repetition show you?

Look up the definition for "wormwood." How does this definition help you to understand Amos 5:7 better?

Meditate on Amos 5:24. List the ways that justice and righteousness in abundance are good for us. Think about how we have received them in the gospel!

Amos 7-9

The ending of the book of Amos brings warnings of judgment and the promise of a Redeemer.

The prophet has a series of visions. As Amos sees a vision of a destructive swarm of locusts coming upon the people of Israel, He intercedes and asks that the Lord would not bring Israel to a place they could not recover from (Hosea 7:2, 5). Amos sounds vaguely like Abraham pleading for any righteous people who lived in the wicked town of Sodom and Gomorrah before the Lord destroyed it (Genesis 18:16-33). Amaziah, Bethel's priest and Israel's spiritual leader, told King Jeroboam that Amos was conspiring against the king. The priest obviously rejected Amos's prophecies, and thus further judgment was set by the Lord. Amos's treatment reminds us of how the Pharisees and Sadducees will reject Jesus and turn Him over to Rome (Matthew 27:1-2). Jesus will be the final Prophet and Priest, for He declares the Word of God and offers Himself as the final and all-sufficient sacrifice for the sins of God's people, thus obliterating the need for the priests and the sacrificial system. Jesus's message will not be well received, even though it is a message that brings true hope and life.

In Amos 8, Amos warned of the bitter judgment and destruction that would come because the people refused to heed the Lord. The prophet told the people that they would suffer a physical death and no longer hear the Word of the Lord (Amos 8:3, 11-12). No one can hide from the Lord. This should cause us to have a proper fear and respect for Him. No evil or injustice is unnoticed by Him, and He will have the final say. And yet, even with these strong messages of judgment, there was also a message of hope. The last five verses of Amos look forward to the day when all that is wrong will be made right. More importantly, these verses point to the One who would come as the Messiah for all of Israel and the world (Amos 9:11-15). Jesus is the promised Messiah. He has come with the power to redeem even the most broken things, and we are covered by His righteousness.

"He has come with the power to redeem even the most broken things."

QUESTIONS

We see the Lord "relent" His punishment toward His people multiple times in chapter 7. What does this tell us about His character?

Meditate on the last two verses of this book. In what ways does this offer hope amid the struggle of judgment?

Now that you have finished reading the book of Amos, what are some of the main themes that carry throughout the book?

There will
be a
deliverance.

Obadiah

GENRE: *Prophet, Pre-exilic*

AUTHOR / DATE WRITTEN

Obadiah • c. 848-840 BC

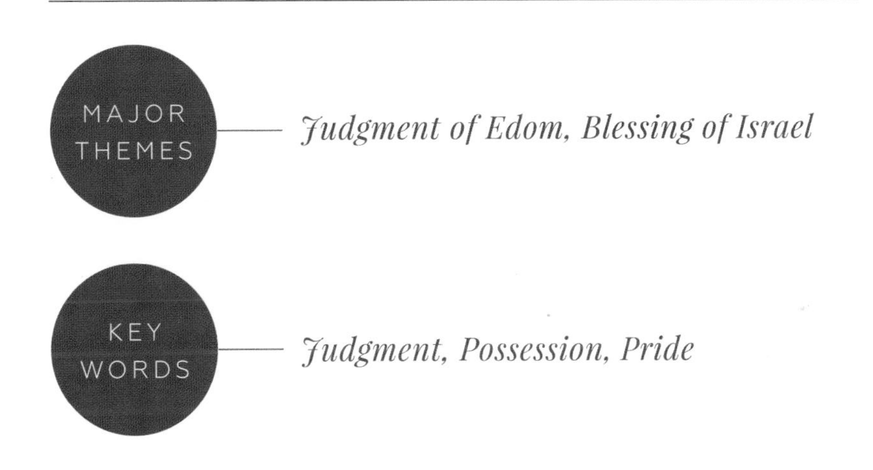

KEY VERSE

OBADIAH 1:17

But there will be a deliverance on Mount Zion, and it will be holy; the house of Jacob will dispossess those who dispossessed them.

Obadiah

The book of Obadiah is the shortest Old Testament book, and yet it is full of truth about God's judgment of sin and the deliverance of His people.

"We can take comfort in knowing that He will be faithful, and He will reign forever."

The book focuses on the nation of Edom that was founded by Jacob's brother, Esau. The nation had been at odds with God's people for generations. Edom's most recent crime against God's people had occurred during the Babylonian invasion. When Jerusalem and the cities of Judah were invaded, Edom plundered the cities and even captured and killed some of their refugees. The book of Obadiah reminds us that God is sovereign in the affairs of men. Nations rise and fall at His command. The nation of Edom had grown strong. In their pride, they believed that nothing could hurt them (Obadiah 3). However, God in His justice would judge their sin.

Obadiah presents Edom's pride and subsequent fall as a picture of the pride and fall of all nations and people. Edom was not the only nation that was prideful. Pride has affected all human beings since they were born. And if we follow in the footsteps of Edom, indulging in our pride and placing ourselves in a higher position than we ought to, we will meet the same end. No nation or person is self-sufficient. We all depend on God's mercy to give us breath each day. Praise the Lord that He delivers us from our pride and gives us new hearts that can see and understand the truth of the gospel.

The nation of Edom was against God's people, and God would be faithful to deliver His people and defeat their enemies. In the same way, God will deliver us from our enemies. In fact, He has already delivered us from the enemies of sin and death through the cross of Christ, and He will one day put all the enemies of His people under His feet. The end of the book of Obadiah gives us a glorious promise that the Lord's kingdom will be established. We can take comfort in knowing that He will be faithful, and He will reign forever.

QUESTIONS

Reread Obadiah verse 3. What does this teach you about the effects of pride in our lives?

In what ways does the book of Obadiah give us hope today? What does it teach us about God?

What are some of the major themes you see in the book of Obadiah?

You heard my voice.

Jonah

GENRE: *Prophet, Pre-exilic, Narrative*

AUTHOR / DATE WRITTEN

Jonah • c. 790 BC

Being Faithful to the Call of God, Maintaining a Righteous Attitude

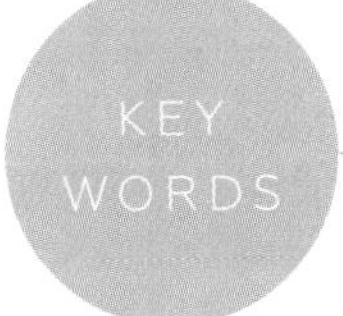

Repentance, Obedience, Anger

KEY VERSE

JONAH 2:2

I called to the Lord in my distress, and he answered me. I cried out for help from deep inside Sheol; you heard my voice.

Jonah 1-4

The book of Jonah is a short story about a rebellious prophet who runs from God.

In the first verses of the book, the Lord tells Jonah to go to Nineveh, the capital of Assyria. Assyria was one of Israel's greatest enemies, and the Lord eventually uses Assyria to conquer Israel and bring them into exile for judgment for their sin. When Jonah hears God's call, he boards a ship that is heading in the opposite direction of Nineveh. God gives Jonah clear directions, but Jonah did not want to obey, so he attempts to run away from God by taking a ship to Tarshish. When Jonah is on the ship, God sends a great storm to prohibit Jonah's voyage. As Jonah lays sleeping on the ship, he wakes up to frantic sailors fearing for their lives and wondering what they can do to survive. As they cast lots to see who is responsible for bringing about this mighty storm, the lot falls on Jonah. The pagan sailors know that Jonah has sinned by running from God, and they ask the prophet what they must do. Jonah tells them to hurl him into the sea because he is the reason behind the storm. In His mercy, God allows Jonah to be swallowed by a great fish. He spends three days and three nights in its belly before being spit out. Now, Jonah finally goes to Nineveh as God told him to do. God had given Jonah another chance.

When Jonah tells the people of Nineveh about the coming judgment of God, the people repent immediately. Unlike Jonah, they desire to obey the Lord. Jonah's heart is merciless and stubborn toward the people. He was bitter and angry that God showed mercy to them, and he tells the Lord that this was why he ran in the first place. He knew God was compassionate and loving, and He would extend His forgiveness to the evil people in Nineveh (Jonah 4:2). The Lord questions Jonah's anger and asks why He should not care for a city of many people. As God questions Jonah, we must also ask this question of ourselves. Like Jonah, are we hard-hearted against those we consider enemies? Do we desire that all men be saved and know the truth of the gospel?

The book of Jonah offers us many pictures of Christ. The great storm that stops Jonah from running away reminds us of the storm Jesus encountered when He was on the Sea of Galilee with His disciples (Mark 4:35-41). The disciples were fearful and panicking, just like the pagan sailors. However, Jesus offered a much different solution than what Jonah experienced. Instead of casting Himself into the sea as a sacrifice, Jesus tells the sea to be still. He is not like Jonah, the prophet rebelling against God. He is the great and final prophet

"... unworthy of God's grace but chosen by Him to be saved and redeemed nonetheless."

because He is God in the flesh. Jesus would eventually offer His life as a sacrifice on the cross, fulfilling the sign of Jonah. Jesus tells the Pharisees that just as Jonah was hidden in the belly of the whale, so He will be in the "heart of the earth" for three days and three nights (Matthew 12:40). Jesus is pointing to His death and resurrection. And while the people of Nineveh repented over the message of the Lord from Jonah, the religious leaders and Jews would not repent over Jesus's message, and what He said was far greater than what Jonah said. The message of Jonah gives us glimpses of Christ, and it will be a story He will use to rebuke the religious leaders of the day who were as stubborn as the prophet who refused to have compassion toward people who were lost. May we learn from Jonah's story, and may we see ourselves as the people of Nineveh, unworthy of God's grace but chosen by Him to be saved and redeemed nonetheless.

QUESTIONS

Meditate on Jonah 3:10. How does this communicate to you the importance of fleeing from sin?

What does Jonah teach you about the importance of humility and obedience to the Lord?

What are some ways that you can identify with Jonah?

He delights
in faithful
love.

Micah

GENRE: *Prophet, Pre-exilic, Narrative*

AUTHOR / DATE WRITTEN

Micah • c. 740-700 BC

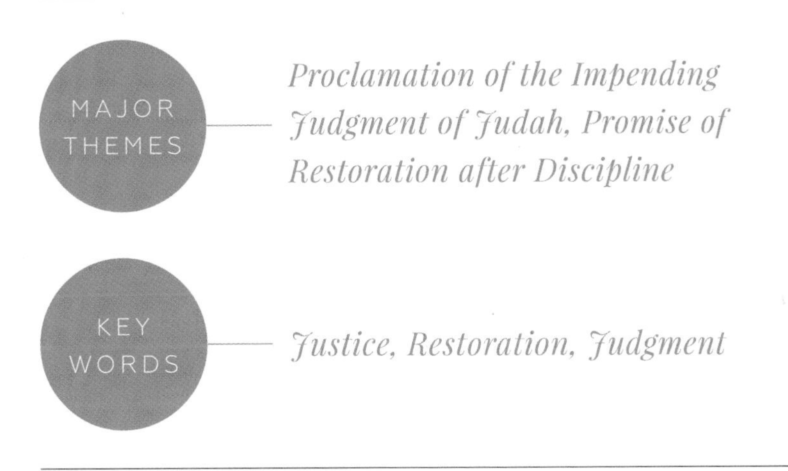

KEY VERSES

MICAH 7:18-19

Who is a God like you, forgiving iniquity and passing over rebellion for the remnant of his inheritance? He does not hold on to his anger forever because he delights in faithful love. He will again have compassion on us; he will vanquish our iniquities. You will cast all our sins into the depths of the sea.

Micah 1-3

The prophet Micah lived around the same time as the prophet Isaiah when the people of Israel were split into the northern and southern kingdoms.

The Lord gives Micah three sermons to preach in an attempt to open the eyes of the people and call them to return to the Lord. Micah opens each divine message with a command for the people to "hear." Micah pleaded with the people to hear the words that God spoke, and he laments over their unwillingness to repent (Micah 1:8-9). The people of Samaria and Judah would soon be brought under judgment from foreign nations because of it. Jesus will follow in Micah's footsteps and lament for the city of Jerusalem, who would not repent again during His time on earth (Luke 19:41-44). Jerusalem would again face destruction after Christ's ascension when the Romans destroyed the city in 70 AD.

At the beginning of chapter 2, Micah specifically calls out those who oppressed and seized the property of others. They would have no place in the assembly of the Lord that would eventually be gathered back to the land after their punishment and exile. Micah also prophesies judgment against false prophets who told the people that they would experience blessing, even though they were wicked and disobeyed God's commands. One day, the Lord would bring His faithful, remnant hope in exile, and He would lead them faithfully and care for them as a shepherd cares for his flock. The Lord even mentions a king who would be set over the people. This is foreshadowing Christ, the Shepherd King, who comes to earth to provide salvation for the people of God and tenderly leads and cares for them.

Jesus would be much different than the civil leaders and rulers of Judah and Israel who hate good and love evil. They did not act out the justice and righteousness of God. Jesus is the only King and leader who is perfectly righteous and just. He sought out the oppressed, the poor, and those who have been wronged, and He brought them the message of salvation. He gave them true hope and eternal life. During Micah's time, the false prophets and evil leaders were unconcerned about the sin of the nation because they were God's chosen

"God's grace should push us to be holy as He is holy."

people. They thought they were protected from any kind of punishment. They took advantage of the grace of God. Their actions would lead to Jerusalem's eventual destruction. It is the same for those who believe that their sin will not have any consequence. Those who rebel against the Lord will face destruction. Believers of Jesus must carefully watch and observe that they do not take advantage of God's grace toward them (Galatians 5:13). Sin must not be our friend. It will wreak havoc on our lives and draw us away from spiritual growth and joy in the Lord. God's grace should push us to be holy as He is holy (1 Peter 1:16).

QUESTIONS

Focus on Micah's plea for Israel to listen and pay attention. Do you feel comfortable and confident in listening to the Lord and paying attention to His commands?

What do these chapters teach us about the foolishness of opposing God?

Spend some time reflecting on what is "just." How does our understanding of the character of God inform the way that we define "justice"?

Micah 4-7

As Micah's second message continues, we are overwhelmed by promises of hope that follow the warnings of judgment.

"A life lived apart from Jesus will end in emptiness, but a life lived for Him will be full."

God was pleading through the prophet Micah for His people to return. He would rescue and redeem them as they turned to Him, and He gave them a glimpse of the promised hope. In chapter 4, the Lord reveals that Jerusalem would one day be a place that He would lift up and allow many people from all across the world to come and learn and walk in the ways of God. This is the believer's inheritance and is a picture of the New Jerusalem, our heavenly home. While we belong to this kingdom now as followers of Christ, we will one day physically live in it with Jesus reigning as King. Micah gives a glorious prophecy of Christ's coming by saying that the Messiah would come from Bethlehem to deliver His people and shepherd the nation (Micah 5:1-5). The description is fulfilled by Christ, though His arrival in Bethlehem would be less glorious than the people anticipated. Jesus, the King of the universe, would be born as a baby in a lowly manger. He would be a King unlike any other king the world had ever known or will ever know, and He would bring everlasting peace.

The last message of Micah is a reminder of what God desires from sinners. Chapter 6 begins with the Lord bringing "a case" against His people for their sins. He also questions their unbelief and rebellion against Him (Micah 6:2). In the midst of His judgment, the Lord tells His people what He requires of them in Micah 6:8. It is a heavily quoted verse, but the kind of life the Lord describes here is a depiction of the perfect life of Christ. Jesus embodies justice, kindness, and humility. As we are joined to Him through the gospel, He sanctifies us and leads us into this kind of life as well. The following verses of chapter 6 hold more judgment for the wicked of Samaria and Judah. They will face desolation for their sins (Micah 6:13). This is the end of any person who does not follow Christ. A life lived apart from Jesus will end in emptiness, but a life lived for Him will be full. The book of Micah ends with the promise of the faithfulness of our God. Though His people would see destruction and exile, He would deliver them and bring them home. He would forgive their sins and cast their sins "into the depths of the sea" (Micah 7:19). We can place our hope in Him and be confident that He will never fail His people.

QUESTIONS

Meditate on Micah 4:5. What are practical ways that we walk in the name of the Lord?

Paraphrase Micah 7:14-20 in your own words.

What is something God has taught you through the reading of Micah?

great in power

Nahum

GENRE: *Prophet, Pre-exilic*

AUTHOR / DATE WRITTEN

Nahum • c. 640–612 BC

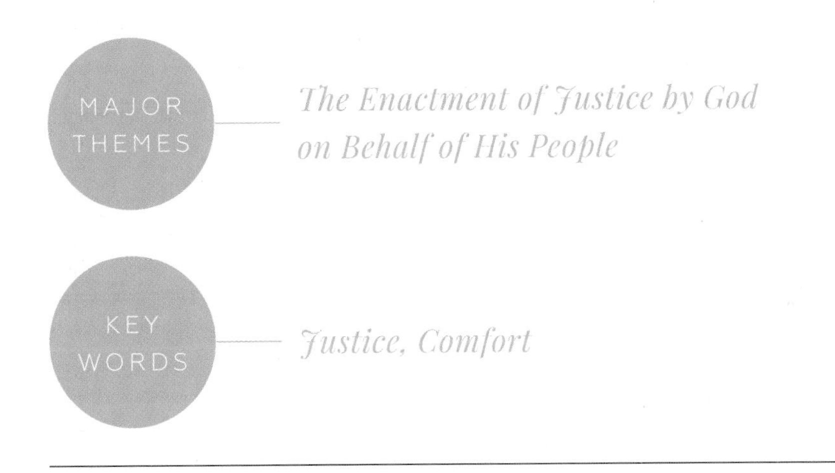

The Enactment of Justice by God on Behalf of His People

Justice, Comfort

KEY VERSE

NAHUM 1:3

The Lord is slow to anger but great in power; the Lord will never leave the guilty unpunished. His path is in the whirlwind and storm, and clouds are the dust beneath his feet.

Nahum 1-3

The prophet Nahum wrote the book of Nahum, and it chronicles the judgment that would come to the evil city of Nineveh in Assyria.

"We can be confident that our God will do what is right, and He will not let evil go unanswered."

God, in His long-suffering and mercy, had given the people a chance to repent generations before when He sent Jonah to them. At that time, they had repented. But now, years later, they had gone back to their sin. They threatened God's people, took part in evil rituals, and were violent and ascribed little value to human life. God would judge their wickedness and would protect His people.

In the first chapter, Nahum describes the Lord's vengeance against His enemies but actually makes no mention of the people of Assyria. This chapter reminds us that God is slow to anger and that He will not pardon the guilty who do not repent. He is gracious and merciful, but when the Lord sees evil, He will require justice. This passage should encourage and calm us. We live in a world full of brokenness and evil, and though sometimes we wonder why the Lord allows tragic and horrible things to happen, we can rest in the knowledge that He avenges wrongdoing. Praise God that He has saved us from our own evilness and brokenness, and He has covered us in His righteousness. Without His intervention through the gospel, we would face the same judgment as the people of Assyria.

Chapter 2 provides details of the collapse of Nineveh. It is a shocking devastation to the city, and its destruction is total and complete. While reading this chapter, we can easily see Nineveh as a parallel to all of those who reject the Lord. Some carry on in rebellion against God, and while it may seem like He does not respond, His ultimate response and judgment are coming. In the same chapter, the Lord tells Nineveh that He is bringing destruction to the wicked city but restoration to His people (Nahum 2:2). This should point to the last days of the world when all evil will be destroyed in Christ's return, but the people of God will be gathered and secured forever.

The book closes with a list of offenses the Lord brings against the people of Nineveh, "the city of blood" (Nahum 3:1). While they have committed atrocities against other nations and even within their own walls, the root of their sin was setting themselves up as higher than any other nation or God (Nahum 3:8-17). The Lord would humble them, and He would deliver the

nations from their evil. Nineveh's fall represents the fall of all people who reject God. God is long-suffering and compassionate, but there is a day coming when there will no longer be any opportunity to repent. We must give our insecurity over sharing the gospel to the Lord and tell others of the good news of Christ. The Lord will use our evangelism to soften people's hearts and minds toward the good news of Jesus Christ. Nahum reminds us that God is good, and He is a stronghold in times of trouble (Naham 1:7). He is good, gracious, and loving, as well as just, holy, and jealous. We can be confident that our God will do what is right, and He will not let evil go unanswered.

QUESTIONS

What does Nahum 1:2 mean when it calls God "jealous and avenging"?

How does this book grow your trust in God?

What are some examples of God's long-suffering in this book?

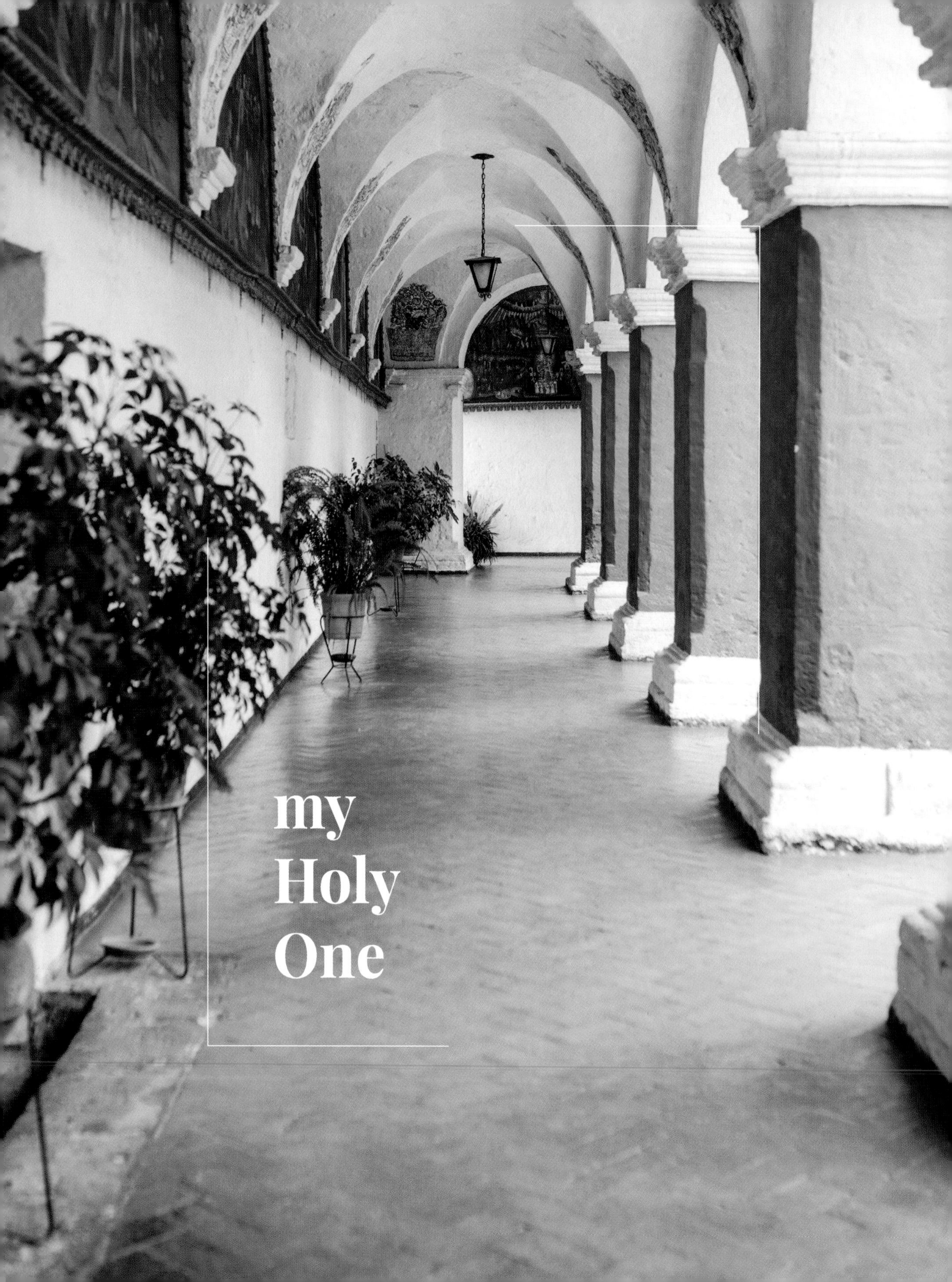

my Holy One

Habakkuk

GENRE: *Prophet, Pre-exilic*

AUTHOR / DATE WRITTEN

Habakkuk • c. 605–597 BC

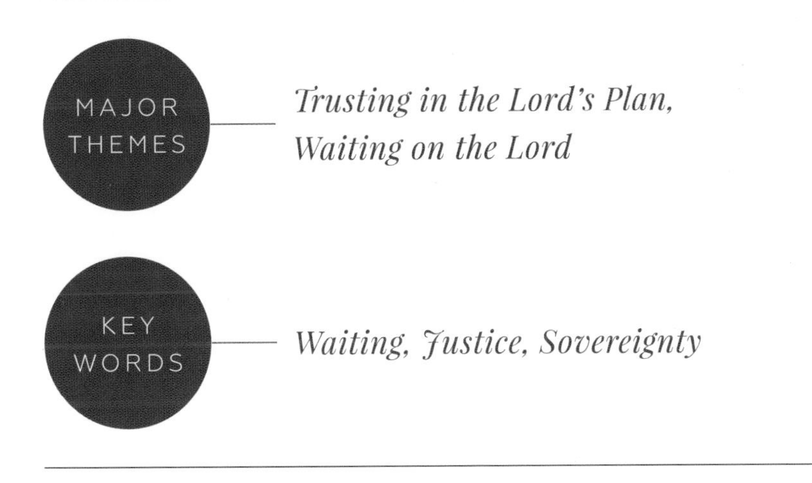

Trusting in the Lord's Plan, Waiting on the Lord

Waiting, Justice, Sovereignty

KEY VERSE

HABAKKUK 1:12

Are you not from eternity, Lord my God? My Holy One, you will not die. Lord, you appointed them to execute judgment; my Rock, you destined them to punish us.

Habakkuk 1-3

The small book of Habakkuk is full of rich and encouraging truth for believers.

Habakkuk lived in the southern kingdom of Judah and saw God's people become like other wicked nations. In the first chapter of the book, Habakkuk cries out to the Lord about injustice being unanswered. He saw that God's chosen people were rebelling against Him and hurting those who were faithful to God, and he wondered why the Lord seemed to do nothing about it. Habakkuk is brutally honest with the Lord, and the Lord was quick to respond to him. The Lord told the prophet, as we saw in Isaiah, Jeremiah, and Ezekiel, that because of Judah's sin, they would be enslaved by the Babylonians (Habakkuk 1:6).

Habakkuk then questions the Lord again. As you read his words, you can easily see he is overwhelmed by the thought of a nation as evil as the Babylonians being used by the Lord to judge His people. Habakkuk's doubts and fears are on full display as he approaches God, but the prophet also ends with words of trust in the Lord. His account of lament for the nation and cries to God are so helpful for us to read. Habakkuk lives the reality of every human being in a broken world. We are overwhelmed with the effects of evil all around us, but we know that we are secure in Christ. Our God is a great refuge and stronghold for His people; "He will never allow the righteous to be shaken" (Psalm 55:22).

Habakkuk 2:4 is one of the most well-known phrases in Scripture: the righteous shall live by faith (ESV). The verse is quoted three times in the New Testament (Romans 1:17, Galatians 3:11, Hebrews 10:38). In Habakkuk 2, the Lord reminds the prophet that even though he could not see everything the Lord was doing, he could trust Him and that while evil may seem to be undefeated, it would never win. Babylon would have to answer to the Lord for their sin. The Lord promised a day where instead of the earth being filled with evil, it would be filled with His glory. When Jesus returns, He will bring God's judgment upon the earth, but He will also fill it with the glory of God (Habakkuk 2:14).

"Our eternal security and peace are in God."

Chapter 3 is Habakkuk's prayer. It shows the depth of his walk with God and reminds us of how we should come before the Lord. The last verses of the book encourage us that we can praise the Lord no matter what we face. Habakkuk praised the Lord when Judah's exile to Babylon loomed overhead, and we can praise Him no matter what we face. We may not understand His plan, and everything may seem hopeless, but our eternal security and peace are in God. He will never change, and He is always victorious.

QUESTIONS

Reflect on Habakkuk 2:1. What are some ways that we can and should wait on the Lord in a similar way to Habakkuk?

Reread Habakkuk 3:17-18. In what ways can this offer you hope and encouragement amid difficulty?

What is the most prominent theme you see in Habakkuk?

Seek
the
Lord.

Zephaniah

GENRE: *Prophet, Pre-exilic, Narrative*

AUTHOR / DATE WRITTEN

Zephaniah • c. 630 BC

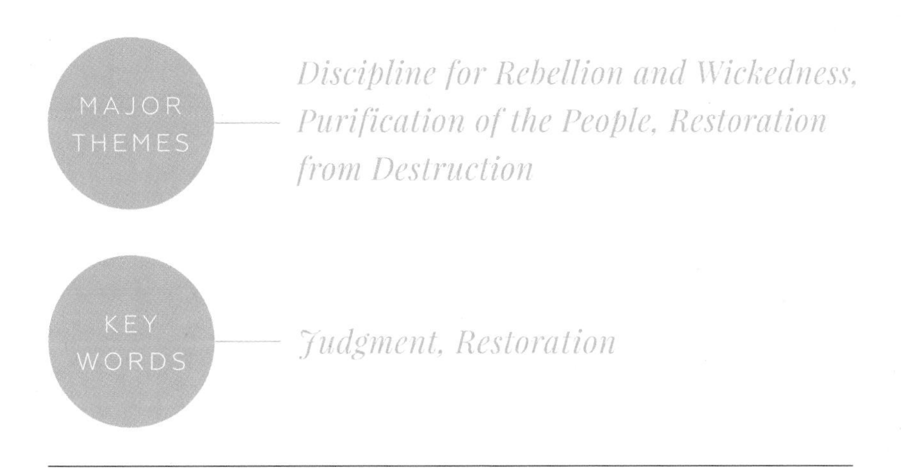

KEY VERSE

ZEPHANIAH 2:3

Seek the Lord, all you humble of the earth, who carry out what he commands. Seek righteousness, seek humility; perhaps you will be concealed on the day of the Lord's anger.

Zephaniah 1-3

The book of Zephaniah is very similar to the book of Joel. Zephaniah focuses on the theme of the "day of the Lord."

In the first chapter, God proclaims His judgment of the land of Judah and the surrounding nations. Judah had rejected the Lord and had sought fulfillment in other gods and pleasures. As God describes His judgment, it is almost as if He is providing a picture of undoing His own creation (Zephaniah 1:3). Nothing would be able to deliver the people from this terrible day. All of the inhabitants of the earth would come to an end (Zephaniah 1:18). And though we can soberly think of the day that unbelievers will face when Christ returns, we can—if we are a follower of Christ—read this chapter in astonishment because we once belonged to the group of people who will one day receive God's wrath. But Jesus stood in our place, and He bore our punishment for sin. Judah would face judgment for rejecting the Lord, but that judgment did not come without the promise that one day all would be made right. The Lord's restoration of Judah points toward our final restoration through Jesus Christ.

In chapter 2, the Lord provides details of His anger for sin against the nations who do not fear Him. All of the nations that exalted themselves and their gods above the Lord would be humbled. All of the world is under the sovereign hand of God, and there are no nations or people more powerful than He is. While we cannot see the justice of the Lord always at work, He will have the final say, and He will not let injustice go unpunished.

Zephaniah 3 beautifully shows that God will one day bring all nations to call upon His name and worship in unity. Israel will be restored. Our God will keep His promises. He will gather His people together, and He will rejoice over them (Zephaniah 3:17). We can be confident that this is who our God is. He does not leave us in our sin, but He comes to rescue and redeem us. He brings us hope, forgiveness, and mercy. He brings us Himself. Our God takes broken things, and He restores them. We can be confident that He will do the same for us.

"He comes to rescue and redeem us."

QUESTIONS

Zephaniah 1 speaks about the wrath God poured out. In what ways is God's wrath a good thing?

What does it look like to seek righteousness and humility as Zephaniah 2:3 says?

In what ways does reading through this book in one sitting help you to pick up on its themes?

Think carefully about your ways.

Haggai

GENRE: *Prophet, Post-exilic*

AUTHOR / DATE WRITTEN

Haggai • c. 520 BC

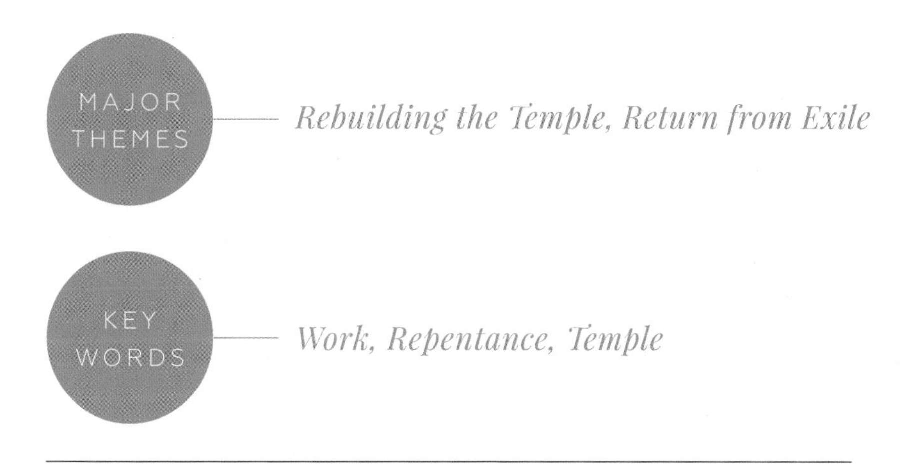

KEY VERSES

HAGGAI 1:5

Now, the Lord of Armies says this:
'Think carefully about your ways...'

Haggai 1-2

The tiny book of Haggai is packed with truth, and it points us to Jesus.

In Haggai, a small portion of Judah had returned to Jerusalem to rebuild the temple. But before they could rebuild the temple, the Lord gives a message to Haggai and His people. The message was that they needed to put the Lord first. They were living as though they were the most important thing. But they had gotten things backward. They built their own houses but neglected the Lord's house. The Lord wanted them to consider their ways and search their hearts. He desired to be present with His people, and the temple was the physical manifestation of His dwelling with them. Haggai reminds the people that if the Lord does not dwell with His people, there is no point in building anything else (Haggai 1:7-9). Jesus will have the utmost regard for the house of His Father. He will even clear the temple of all who seek to use it to take advantage of others (Matthew 21:12-13). And Jesus will eventually allow us to become the temples of the Lord since we have been given the Spirit of God through our salvation (Galatians 2:20). The Lord dwells within His people, and someday we will be physically reunited with God. Haggai's urging for Judah to remember the Lord's dwelling place should cause us to rejoice that the Lord is so intimately present with us.

God chose Zerubbabel to lead the people in obeying the Lord and rebuilding the temple. Though Zerubbabel was in the line of David, he was not a king. He served as a mere governor, but he was faithful. He served the Lord and did what God had called him to do, and God saw his faithfulness. Zerubbabel would not be forgotten, and his name would be recorded in the genealogy of Jesus (Matthew 1:12-13, Luke 3:27). His life was an intricate piece of the story of redemption, all because he was faithful. Zerubabel's obedience to God was a glimmer of hope for the line of David. God had not forgotten His promise to David (2 Samuel 7:12-13), and soon there would be one who would come to Israel who was even greater and more obedient than Zerubbabel. While Zerubbabel's faithfulness allowed the people to worship and dwell with God through a temple, Jesus's faithfulness would give all of His people complete access to the Lord forever.

"The Lord dwells within His people."

QUESTIONS

Spend some time in self-examination in light of Haggai 1:9. What are some ways you tend to yourself better than you tend to glorifying God and obeying His commands?

Reread Haggai 2:19. What does this verse remind you about God's character?

Summarize the overall point of the book of Haggai in your own words.

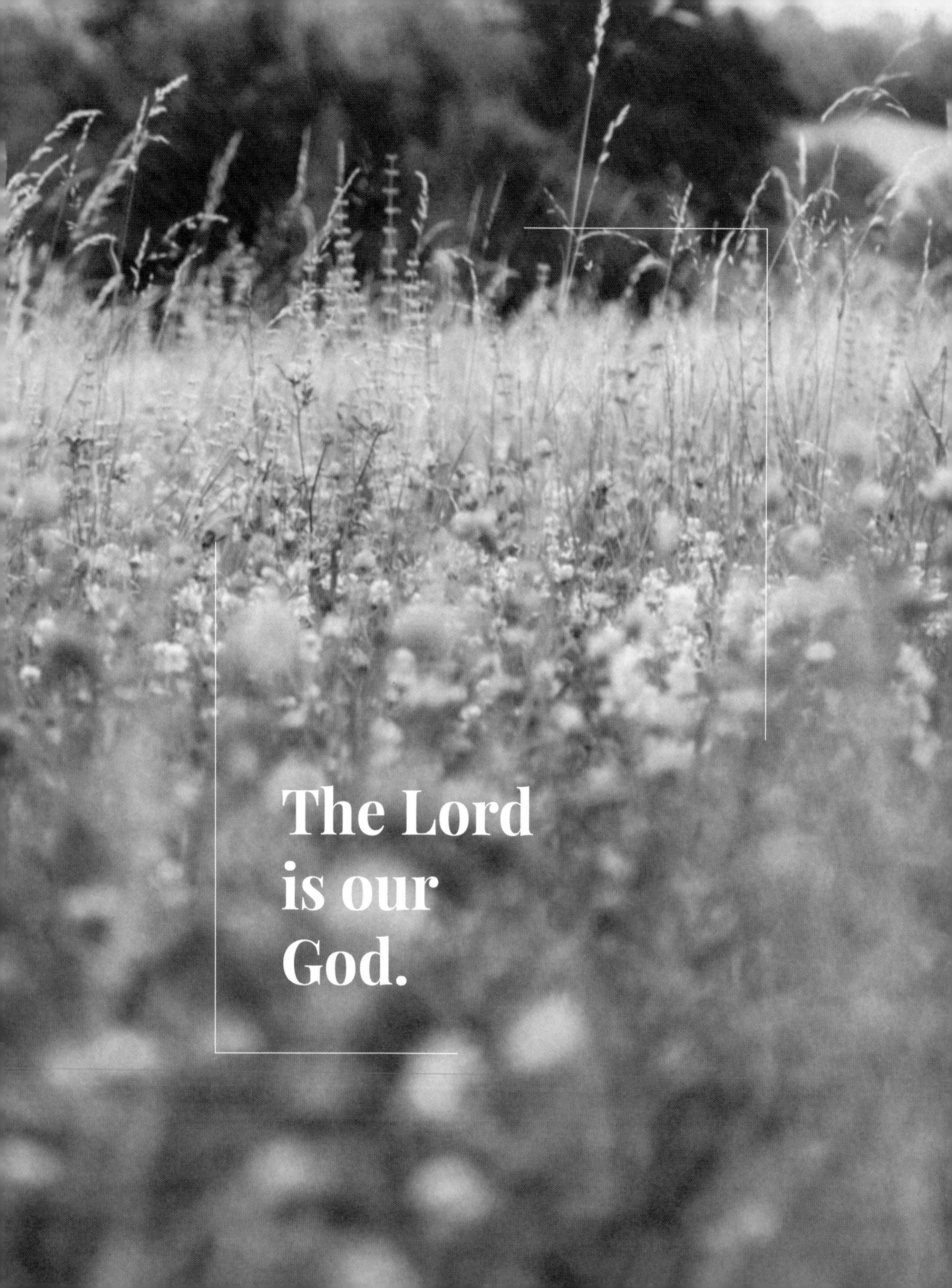
The Lord
is our
God.

Zechariah

GENRE: *Prophet, Post-exilic*

AUTHOR / DATE WRITTEN

Zechariah • c. 518 BC

MAJOR THEMES — *The People of God Maintaining Their Covenant, Awaiting the Messiah*

KEY WORDS — *Repentance, Restoration, Messiah*

KEY VERSE

ZECHARIAH 13:9

I will put this third through the fire; I will refine them as silver is refined and test them as gold is tested. They will call on my name, and I will answer them. I will say: They are my people, and they will say: The Lord is our God.

Zechariah 1-3

The book of Zechariah takes place after the exiles from Babylon return to Jerusalem.

Zechariah was a prophet who served alongside the prophet Haggai. Like Haggai, he encouraged the people to continue rebuilding the temple. The book starts with a call to return. The people needed to repent and then turn from their sin, and the Lord promised that if they returned to Him, He would return to them (Zechariah 1:3). The Lord urged them not to be like their fathers, who did not listen to His instruction and ignored His prophets. And by God's grace, the people did repent and listen, and the Lord would send encouragement through Zechariah's visions to help them persevere in their return from the exile.

Life after the exile was hard for God's people. Everything that had once been was no more, and they were regathering and rebuilding after seventy years in captivity. While the visions of Zechariah are full of wild and vivid imagery, each one contains a comforting message from the Lord toward His people. In Zechariah's first two visions, the Lord is telling His people that His favor has come back upon Jerusalem, and He will establish it and let it be rebuilt (Zechariah 1:16). The vision of the four horns revealed that the nations who scattered the Lord's people would face judgment. The enemies of the people of Judah would not go unpunished (Zechariah 1:21).

Zechariah's vision of a man with a measuring line taking the city's width and length reveals that Jerusalem will be inhabited without walls because the Lord Himself will defend her and be her glory (Zechariah 2:5). And while nations would be punished for their mistreatment of God's people, the city of Jerusalem would someday draw the nations of the world to its doors because of the presence of the Lord (Zechariah 2:11-12).

"God in His mercy would send the Messiah, Jesus, to rescue them."

In chapter 3, we see an incredible vision of the Lord that points to the coming of Jesus, the Great High Priest. Remember, priesthood dates back to Leviticus, where priests began offering sacrifices for people's sins. Jesus is referred to as our Great High Priest because He offered Himself as the perfect and final sacrifice. Zechariah sees the high priest named Joshua. In the vision, Joshua stands before the angel of the Lord with Satan beside him. Satan is accusing Joshua, but the Lord rebukes him. Joshua was wearing filthy gar-

ments, but the Lord cleanses Joshua and gives him clean garments. The Lord tells Joshua that if he walks in the Lord's ways, he will rule over the house of God. And then the Lord mentions His servant, the Righteous Branch (Zechariah 3:8). We have heard this name before when the Lord speaks of the coming Messiah, but the Lord then says the Branch is going to "take away the iniquity of this land in a single day" (Zechariah 3:9). This is the day that Jesus, the final High Priest, will take away the sins of His people by offering His life as a sacrifice on the cross. Though God's people made many mistakes, God in His mercy would send the Messiah, Jesus, to rescue them. God will be faithful to us as well, and we look forward to the day when Jesus will return. But for now, just like the people of Israel in the rebuilding of the temple, we have work to do.

QUESTIONS

Reread Zechariah 1:4-6. How does this inform the way you think about and respond to the Word of God?

How does Zechariah 2:13 expand your understanding of God's holiness?

How do you see God's character highlighted in chapter 3?

Zechariah 4-6

God will always be faithful to His people. The visions of Zechariah are continued in these chapters, and God's everlasting faithfulness is on display.

"Jesus established peace between man and God."

We are reminded that God's Spirit is the key, as Zechariah 4:6 says that it is not by might or power, but only by His Spirit. God uses small things to do big things. The temple that Zerubbabel built seemed small compared to Solomon's, but the things of God are never small, even when they appear that way to our feeble eyes. And the rebuilding of the temple was yet another sign of God's grace and mercy for His people. They had sinned and broken their covenant relationship with Him, but He was allowing them to come near once more. He desired to be with His people.

The vision of the flying scroll and the woman in a basket in chapter 5 reveals how the Lord removes and deals with sin. In the vision of the flying scroll, God's curse against those who reject Him as Lord and live in wickedness is written and carried out. The vision of the woman in the basket shows the iniquity of the people leaving the city and going back to "the land of Shinar" or Babylon (Zechariah 5:10-11). Iniquity would have no place in God's restored city. We know that this vision is ultimately speaking of the heavenly city of Jerusalem, where sin and evil will forever be destroyed. Babylon represents all of the world's evil, so the evil that plagues God's people will be removed and sent to this city. This reminds us of how Christ's sacrifice has allowed for the complete removal of our sins. He took our iniquity upon Himself so that we might be washed clean in His righteousness. We can one day come into the New Jerusalem and be with the Lord for eternity because of Christ.

The vision of the four chariots in chapter 6 also shows us that evil will not be allowed to dwell freely in Babylon with no interference from the Lord. The Lord will send out His forces to deal with nations who are idolatrous and wicked (Zechariah 6:5). God's people will dwell safely and securely in His land, and they will have no reason to fear. As the passage ends, we see that a crown is placed on Joshua's head and then taken off and taken to the temple. This was a symbolic reminder that no earthly king or priest deserved a crown, but one day the King of kings would come and wear the crown. Jesus the Messiah, the Righteous Branch, reigns in faithfulness. He would be both Priest and King, and He would build the temple of the Lord through His own body (Hebrews 7). Jesus established peace between man and God (Romans 5:1).

QUESTIONS

Reread Zechariah 4:10. What are some other instances in which you can think of small things or "small" people that God has used to accomplish His will?

What symbolism do you find helpful for your understanding of chapter 5?

How does reading chapter 6 aid your understanding of the symbolism in chapter 5?

Zechariah 7-10

In chapter 7, the people have questions about which fasts they should continue to keep since some of the things for which they have fasted came to fruition.

They had returned to Jerusalem from exile and were rebuilding the temple. However, God wanted the people to focus on their hearts for Him and not just the outward rules. The people were beginning to focus too much on religious traditions and feasts while their hearts were far from the Lord. The Lord gave the people an example of the kind of obedience He desired. He wanted them to love justice, mercy, and compassion and for them not to oppress others (Zechariah 7:8-10). He described how their ancestors had not listened to His call to repentance, so they had been scattered. But in chapter 8, the Lord reminded His people of how He has returned to Jerusalem and brought peace. He ordained that their fasting be turned into times of feasting and celebration. One day, this peace will be fully restored when Jesus returns to earth and gathers His people together. Our fasting and mourning in this broken creation will be replaced with feasting as we embark on the beginning of a new journey in Christ's kingdom.

These chapters are full of promises of Jesus, the coming Messiah. His triumphal entry is predicted in Zechariah 9:9. The King of Zion (Zion is the heavenly city of God) would one day enter Jerusalem with righteousness and salvation, and He would be seated on a donkey. He would be the one true King, unlike any other king in the world. His entry into Jerusalem, the city of God, shows us His humility. Zechariah later describes Christ's second coming in that He would appear once more, not on a donkey but a fierce warhorse (Zechariah 14, Revelation 19:11-16). When Jesus comes again, He will save His people from evil, and His entry will be glorious (Zechariah 9:14-16). He is described in Zechariah 10:4 as our cornerstone, which is the first stone laid when building a foundation. He is also described as our tent peg, who is safe and secure and on whom we can place the weight of our burdens. Finally, Zechariah writes that He is our battle bow, who is our victorious warrior. The promise is sure, Jesus will come and bring His people home (Zechariah 10:10). No matter what we are facing, we can trust and hope in this eternal truth.

"The promise is sure, Jesus will come and bring His people home."

QUESTIONS

How does this section of reading strengthen your knowledge that God can always bring about redemption?

What does Zechariah 8:6 teach you about God?

Meditate on Zechariah 10:6. How does this verse grow your affection for Christ?

Zechariah 11-14

Repent and return was the message of the previous prophets, and Zechariah's message is the same.

"We have received God's Spirit of mercy and grace through the gospel."

In chapter 11, Zechariah acts out a prophecy of judgment from the Lord to the people. Zechariah acted as the Lord and shepherded a flock that represented Israel. Because of the sins of the people and their "shepherds," God would take favor from them, but He would also take away their union. The three shepherds who were rejected are thought of as the prophets, priests, and kings of Israel, and the union taken away would cause enmity between Judah and Israel. Zechariah represents Christ in this scenario in that the people would reject him, just as they rejected Jesus. When Zechariah asks for his wages for shepherding the flock, he is given thirty pieces of silver. This is the same amount that the religious leaders gave Judas for delivering Jesus to them. Thirty pieces of silver was not a small amount of money, but it was not a great amount either. It was often used as the regular price for a slave. And this is the kind of value God's people would put on the prophets' words.

However, in chapter 12, the tone shifts, and we see the glorious future of Israel, God's chosen people. Our God will pour out His Spirit, a Spirit of grace and mercy, and the people who once rejected Him will repent and return at last. God in His mercy and faithfulness would redeem them. In these verses, God describes Himself as Him "whom they pierced" (Zechariah 12:10). This foreshadows the crucifixion where Jesus took on our sin and died so that all who trust in Him can be saved. This is the gospel, and we have received God's Spirit of mercy and grace through the gospel. Zechariah goes on to describe this Messiah again as the shepherd provided by God but struck down, again referring to the death of Christ (Zechariah 13:7).

But on the day of the Lord, all will change as the humble Messiah becomes the conquering King. Rivers will flow from Jerusalem, and our God will be King over all. And all people who love Him will worship at the temple in Jerusalem and celebrate the feast of tabernacles. As documented throughout the Old Testament, all other feasts will be fulfilled, and they would celebrate the final end of Israel's wandering. God was faithful to redeem His people from exile, and He will be faithful to redeem His people from wandering in the world and return them home.

QUESTIONS

What is the hope for Israel found in this section of the reading?

Think about the symbolism of Jerusalem having rivers. Why might this be significant? (Consider that it is the only ancient city not built by a river!)

Spend some time in reflection. What are some things that convicted you as you read the book of Zechariah?

Return
to me.

Malachi

GENRE: *Prophet, Post-exilic*

AUTHOR / DATE WRITTEN

Malachi • *c. 425 BC*

KEY VERSE

MALACHI 3:7

Since the days of your fathers, you have turned from my statutes; you have not kept them. Return to me, and I will return to you,' says the Lord of Armies.

Malachi 1–2

The last book of the Old Testament is God's final message to His people until John the Baptist comes on the scene to proclaim the Messiah's arrival.

"He loves us still and calls us to repent and return."

The people had been given many chances to turn to the Lord, but they remained stubborn in their sin. The book is called "the oracle," or "the burden," of Malachi, and we can be sure that this message burdened the heart of the prophet. The very first verses of the book record God saying that He has loved His people, and their immediate response was to question how God loved them at all. God had proven His love time and time again. He had chosen them before any other nation and set His love on them though there was nothing special about them. Israel had been given divine favor and grace, but they scoffed at it. They were the ones lacking love for the Lord, and this lack of love was at the heart of the sin in their lives.

Malachi addresses how this lack of love for the Lord had deeply affected the people. The priests, the spiritual leaders of Israel, dishonored the Lord by accepting polluted sacrifices. While they gave their best to the foreign governors in their midst, they ridiculed the altar of God (Malachi 1:8). The Lord told them that He would rather them shut the doors of His temple than half-heartedly worship Him (Malachi 1:10). The Lord had allowed the people of Israel to know Him, the Creator of the universe, but they scorned Him. The Lord's name would be known throughout the nations, and there would be plenty of Gentiles who would come to faith in God because of the gospel, while many Jews would reject the Messiah.

In chapter 2, the Lord rebuked the priests for leading the people astray. They had corrupted the original covenant of Levi. Through His final sacrifice on the cross, Jesus would be the Great High Priest who would lead His people to salvation. He would not scorn the altar of the Lord. He would sacrifice Himself upon it for the sake of all of those who would one day believe in Him. The people of Israel were also breaking the covenant of marriage, which was sacred to the Lord. By doing so, they brought destruction upon their families, and they revealed their lack of respect for what the Lord desired for them. Jesus is our perfect bridegroom who displays marital faithfulness and love to His bride, God's church.

These sins Malachi describes are heavy, but they are also all too common today. We are quick to doubt His love, give our second best, and not honor our commitments. And yet, for Israel and for us today, He loves us still and calls us to repent and return.

QUESTIONS

What are some ways that you might have questioned God's love for you? Bring them before the Lord in prayer today.

Look up the definition for the word "defile." How does this help you to understand the offense of presenting defiled food to God?

Meditate on Malachi 2:17. In what ways do we sometimes misunderstand what God declares good or evil?

Malachi 3-4

God urges His people to return to Him and promises that He will return to them. Chapter 3 begins with a prophecy of two messengers.

The first prophesied messenger is John the Baptist. Jesus affirmed that John was the messenger of the covenant (Matthew 11:7-15). The second messenger is the Lord Himself. Jesus, God in the flesh, would come to the temple, and He would act like a refiner for the people's sins. He came to free us from sin and make us like Himself.

God made it clear to the people that they were guilty of robbing Him. They had promised to give to the Lord, and then they did not. They even neglected what they were required to give. God pleaded with them to do right and also reminded them that they were not only robbing God but themselves. They were missing out on God's blessing. They looked to material wealth for security when the Lord wanted them to rely on Him instead. He is the God of abundance who seeks to meet our needs (Malachi 3:10). Scripture does not promise us as believers prosperity for serving God, but there are blessings for faithfulness and obedience to the Lord. Putting our ultimate security in Him and giving back to Him what is His to begin with shows our reliance, trust, and love for Him. What we have is not our own. It all belongs to the Lord.

In all the despair over Israel's faithlessness, the Lord still promises to remember His faithful remnant. In every generation of Israel, there would always be some who loved and feared God. This remnant of Israel would continue, and the Messiah would come from their line. We are reminded that God sees the faithful. There is judgment for sin and rebellion, but there are blessings for faithfulness. God sees the faithfulness of His people, and He will never forget them.

"God sees the faithful."

The Old Testament closes with one more reminder of the day of the Lord. This day would be fulfilled when Jesus would arrive as the great refiner, but it will ultimately be fulfilled at the end of all days when Jesus returns. He will destroy the wicked, but for those who love Him, they will be like cattle leaping as they are released from their stalls. His return will bring us great joy because He will come in righteousness with healing peace. We will finally be with Him and free from the curse, just as God promised Adam and Eve

in Genesis 3:15. The book closes by reminding the people to remember the law of Moses and then to watch for the prophet Elijah. Moses represents all of the Law, and Elijah represents all of the prophets, and Jesus would be the fulfillment of all of the Law and everything the prophets spoke. But for now, for four hundred years, there is silence until Christ burst onto the scene and changes everything.

QUESTIONS

In what ways do we tend to rob God? How do we flee from that behavior?

How can the promise of sending John the Baptist, and then the fulfillment of that promise before Christ's birth, give us hope and encouragement today? If you are unfamiliar with the story of John the Baptist, read Luke 1:5-25 for more information.

How does the ending of the book of Malachi cause you to anticipate Christ's coming?

What is the Gospel?

THANK YOU FOR READING AND ENJOYING THIS STUDY WITH US!
WE ARE ABUNDANTLY GRATEFUL FOR THE WORD OF GOD, THE INSTRUCTION WE GLEAN FROM IT, AND THE EVER-GROWING UNDERSTANDING IT PROVIDES FOR US OF GOD'S CHARACTER. WE ARE ALSO THANKFUL THAT SCRIPTURE CONTINUALLY POINTS TO ONE THING IN INNUMERABLE WAYS: THE GOSPEL.

We remember our brokenness when we read about the fall of Adam and Eve in the garden of Eden (Genesis 3), when sin entered into a perfect world and maimed it. We remember the necessity that something innocent must die to pay for our sin when we read about the atoning sacrifices in the Old Testament. We read that we have all sinned and fallen short of the glory of God (Romans 3:23) and that the penalty for our brokenness, the wages of our sin, is death (Romans 6:23). We all are in need of grace and mercy, but most importantly, we all need a Savior.

We consider the goodness of God when we realize that He did not plan to leave us in this dire state. We see His promise to buy us back from the clutches of sin and death in Genesis 3:15. And we see that promise accomplished with Jesus Christ on the cross. Jesus Christ knew no sin yet became sin so that we might become righteous through His sacrifice (2 Corinthians 5:21). Jesus was tempted in every way that we are and lived sinlessly. He was reviled yet still yielded Himself for our sake, that we may have life abundant in Him. Jesus lived the perfect life that we could not live and died the death that we deserved.

The gospel is profound yet simple. There are many mysteries in it that we can never exhaust this side of heaven, but there is still overwhelming weight to its implications in this life. The gospel is the telling of our sinfulness and God's goodness, and this gracious gift compels a response. We are saved by grace through faith, which means

that we rest with faith in the grace that Jesus Christ displayed on the cross (Ephesians 2:8-9). We cannot save ourselves from our brokenness or do any amount of good works to merit God's favor, but we can have faith that what Jesus accomplished in His death, burial, and resurrection was more than enough for our salvation and our eternal delight. When we accept God, we are commanded to die to our self and our sinful desires and live a life worthy of the calling we have received (Ephesians 4:1). The gospel compels us to be sanctified, and in so doing, we are conformed to the likeness of Christ Himself. This is hope. This is redemption. This is the gospel.

SCRIPTURE TO REFERENCE:

GENESIS 3:15	*I will put hostility between you and the woman, and between your offspring and her offspring. He will strike your head, and you will strike his heel.*
ROMANS 3:23	*For all have sinned and fall short of the glory of God.*
ROMANS 6:23	*For the wages of sin is death, but the gift of God is eternal life in Christ Jesus our Lord.*
2 CORINTHIANS 5:21	*He made the one who did not know sin to be sin for us, so that in him we might become the righteousness of God.*
EPHESIANS 2:8-9	*For you are saved by grace through faith, and this is not from yourselves; it is God's gift—not from works, so that no one can boast.*
EPHESIANS 4:1	*Therefore I, the prisoner in the Lord, urge you to walk worthy of the calling you have received,*

Thank you for studying God's Word with us!

CONNECT WITH US

@thedailygraceco

@kristinschmucker

CONTACT US

info@thedailygraceco.com

SHARE

#thedailygraceco

#lampandlight

VISIT US ONLINE

www.thedailygraceco.com

MORE DAILY GRACE

The Daily Grace App

Daily Grace Podcast